LEEDS POLYTECH

To Renew give the

nade by

e ret

UBU ROI:

AN ANALYTICAL STUDY

JUDITH COOPER

UBU ROI:

AN ANALYTICAL STUDY

TULANE STUDIES IN ROMANCE
LANGUAGES AND LITERATURE
Number 6, 1974

TULANE STUDIES IN ROMANCE LANGUAGES AND LITERATURE
NUMBER 6, 1974

Published by

Department of French and Italian
Department of Spanish and Portuguese

TULANE UNIVERSITY

PRICE $4.00

Please address all inquiries and orders to the Editor, Newcomb College,
Tulane University, New Orleans, Louisiana, 70118
Prices subject to change without notice.

PRINTED IN SPAIN

IMPRESO EN ESPAÑA

I.S.B.N.: 0-912788-05-4

DEPÓSITO LEGAL: V. 2.228 - 1974

ARTES GRÁFICAS SOLER, S. A. — JÁVEA, 28 — VALENCIA (8) — 1974

CONTENTS

	Pages
PREFACE	9
INTRODUCTION	15
CHAPTER I. HISTORICAL BACKGROUND	23
II. PLOT STRUCTURE AND EPISODES	47
III. UBU, THE COMIC TYPE	59
IV. LE PARLER UBU	75
CONCLUSION	105
BIBLIOGRAPHY	113
INDEX	119

PREFACE

Ubu Roi by Alfred Jarry has been increasingly recognized as a play which has had an influence on the entire modern theater and which, more specifically, was an important precursor of the contemporary avant-garde theater in France. In spite of this fact, no one has yet made a complete analysis of the play itself, an analysis which is necessary for any evaluation of it as a work of art and any evaluation of its true place in literary history.

The early criticism of *Ubu Roi* was either vehemently partisan or virulently opposed to the play. This tendency to controversy and partiality has continued throughout much of the criticism of the play. In fact, the largest body of criticism on *Ubu* centers around the controversy over Jarry's authorship of it, a controversy raised in 1921 by Charles Chassé in a pamphlet entitled "Sous le masque d'Alfred Jarry (?). Les Sources d'Ubu-Roi." [1]

The first full-length work on Jarry [2] was written by his close friend Madame Rachilde, wife of Alfred Vallette, the publisher of *Le Mercure de France,* and herself a well-known woman of letters. Her work consists primarily of her own personal recollections of Jarry. Her treatment of *Ubu Roi* follows this same pattern and concentrates on a description of the turbulent events of the opening night of the play at which she

---

[1] Later published along with an essay on the painter Rousseau under the collective title *Dans les coulisses de la gloire, d'Ubu-Roi au Douanier Rousseau* (Paris: Editions de la Nouvelle Revue Critique, n. d.).

[2] Rachilde [Marguerite Eymery Vallette], *Alfred Jarry ou le surmâle de lettres* ("La Vie de Bohème"; Paris: Bernard Grasset, 1928).

was present. Paul Chauveau's book on Jarry[3] was a more complete and scholarly work although it, too, was primarily biographical. His treatment of *Ubu Roi* also includes a lengthy account of the *première* with only a brief discussion of the play itself. Fernand Lot's short work[4] which appeared two years later merely reviewed the basic facts of Jarry's life and work.

There was a general decline in scholarship on Jarry and *Ubu* in the late thirties and early forties, the years immediately preceding and during World War II. After the war, however, critics began to look at Ubu with new eyes; the grotesque figure of Ubu no longer seemed so unreal after the atrocities committed by Hitler. In fact Ubu began to seem prophetic. In France, the renewed interest in Jarry's work was evidenced by the founding of the Collège de 'Pataphysique, an elite group of writers and critics whose goal is to propagate Jarry's sardonic vision of the world. The *Cahiers* and *Dossiers* published by the Collège contain numerous articles on *Ubu Roi* and the other Ubu plays which are quite valuable although their interest is primarily historical.

The most satisfactory single study of Alfred Jarry and his work is the two-chapter study of Professor Roger Shattuck,[5] one of the few Americans who has the honor of being a member of the Collège de 'Pataphysique. Professor Shattuck's study on Jarry centers on an effort to correlate his controversial life and personality with his varied and uneven body of literary creations. His discussion of *Ubu* covers the pertinent biographical and historical facts and summarizes the major aspects of the play. Although his interpretations of individual aspects of the play are often penetrating, in particular his observations on the figure of Ubu, Professor Shattuck's discussion of the play does not constitute a complete analysis.

Since Professor Shattuck's study, we find an ever growing interest in the play and an attempt to re-evaluate its importance in the development of the theater of the twentieth century. Martin Esslin was among the first scholars to recognize *Ubu Roi* as a precursor of the avant-garde theater of the fifties and sixties which he calls "The Theater of the

---

[3] *Alfred Jarry ou la naissance, la vie et la mort du Père Ubu* (Paris: Le Mercure de France, 1932).

[4] *Alfred Jarrry, son œuvre. Portrait et autographe* (Paris: Editions de la Nouvelle Revue Critique, 1934).

[5] In *The Banquet Years, the Arts in France. 1885-1918* (New York: Harcourt, Brace and Company, 1958), pp. 146-194.

Absurd." [6] In concluding his discussion of the play, he states: "And so a play that had only two performances in its first run and evoked a torrent of abuse appears, in the light of subsequent developments, as a landmark and a forerunner." [7] However, since his study concentrates on the later avant-garde dramatists, his discussion of *Ubu Roi* is quite brief.

Two other scholars who have recently recognized the influence of *Ubu* on the contemporary avant-garde theater are Leonard Pronko [8] and George Wellwarth. [9] In their books, both authors are primarily concerned with pointing out the particular aspects of *Ubu Roi* which reappear in the plays of later dramatists such as Eugène Ionesco, Samuel Beckett, and others on whom their studies concentrate. Consequently, their discussions of *Ubu* also remain brief.

Almost every subsequent study of modern drama, and particularly of the Theater of the Absurd, has treated Jarry as an important precursor, if not the actual founder, of the new drama. [10] And yet, the treatment of *Ubu* in these works remains generally superficial.

There have been a few more specialized studies of various aspects of Jarry's work. Jean Morienval included a short discussion of the figure of Ubu in his survey of comic types in French literature. [11] Another study of Ubu's character was made by Johnnie Lou Mathis in her M.A. thesis in which she compared the figures of Ubu and Tartuffe. [12] Mr. A. Carey Taylor has contributed an important preliminary study of

---

[6] *The Theater of the Absurd* (Anchor Books; Garden City, New York: Doubleday and Company, Inc., 1961).

[7] *Ibid.*, p. 258.

[8] In *Avant-Garde: the Experimental Theater in France* (Berkeley and Los Angeles, University of California Press, 1962).

[9] In *The Theater of Protest and Paradox, Developments in the Avant-Garde Drama* (New York: New York University Press, 1964).

[10] The following are among the most important:

Robert Brustein, *The Theater of Revolt* (Boston: Atlantic - Little, Brown and Co., n. d.).

Ruby Cohn, *Currents in Contemporary Drama* (Bloomington: Indiana University Press, 1969).

Geneviève Serreau, *L'Histoire du "nouveau théâtre"* (Idées; Paris: Gallimard, 1966).

[11] *De Pathelin à Ubu, le bilan des types littéraires* (Paris: Librairie Bloud et Gay, n. d.).

[12] "Tartuffe and Ubu" (unpublished M.A. Thesis, University of Tenessee, 1966).

Jarry's vocabulary. [13] Another informative article is that of Ruth B. York on the revival of *Ubu* in 1922. [14] Lewis Franklin Sutton has given a valuable bibliography on Jarry studies up to 1963. [15] There have been several articles on Jarry's work to appear since then. I. Königsberg has contributed to the scholarship on texts that preceded *Ubu*. [16] Manuel Grossman has further discussed Jarry's influence on the Theater of the Absurd. [17] Brian Rainey has related Jarry and *Ubu* to the *fin de siècle* in France. [18] Henri Béhar has examined an aspect of *Ubu enchaîné*. [19] Michel Arrivé has analyzed Jarry's use of sign and symbol. [20] And Jules Bedner has made an excellent study of the *guignolesque* elements in *Ubu*. [21]

In this study, I propose to concentrate entirely on the play *Ubu Roi* in an attempt to analyze and evaluate the comic techniques present in all elements of the play — plot, characterization, and dialogue. Certain biographical and historical facts will be included but only insofar as they are related to the play itself. Jarry's writings on the theater, which help to illuminate the play and which were themselves important in planting the seeds for dramatic renovation, will also be taken into account. In the conclusion, I will then attempt to summarize and evaluate the originality of *Ubu Roi* and to demonstrate why it occupies an important position in the history of the theater in the twentieth century.

I wish to express my deep gratitude to all those whose assistance has made this study possible: to Roger Shattuck for his advice, encourage-

---

[13] "Le Vocabulaire d'Alfred Jarry," *C.A.I.E.F.*, 11 (May, 1959), 307-322.

[14] "Ubu Revisited. The Reprise of 1922," *French Review*, 25, No. 4 (February, 1962), 408-411.

[15] "An Evaluation of Studies on Alfred Jarry from 1894-1963" (unpublished Ph.D. Dissertation, University of North Carolina, 1966).

[16] I. Königsberg, "New Light on Alfred Jarry's Juvenilia," *Modern Language Quarterly*, 27 (September, 1966), 299-305.

[17] Manuel Grossman, "Alfred Jarry and the Theater of the Absurd," *Educational Theater Journal*, 109, No. 4 (December, 1967), 473-477.

[18] Brian E. Rainey, "Alfred Jarry and Ubu: The 'Fin de Siècle' in France," *Wascana Review*, 4 (1969), 28-36.

[19] Henri Béhar, "De l'inversion des signes dans *Ubu enchaîné*," *Etudes Françaises*, 7 (1971), 3-21.

[20] Michel Arrivé, "Structuration et destructuration du signe dans quelques textes de Jarry," in *Essais de sémiotique poétique* (Paris: Larousse, 1972). M. Arrivé is also editing the Pléiade edition of Jarry's *Œuvres*, the first volume of which appeared in 1972. A critical edition of Jarry's work has long been needed.

[21] Jules Bedner, "Eléments guignolesques dans le théâtre d'Alfred Jarry," *Revue d'Histoire Littéraire de la France*, 73 (1973), 69-84.

ment, and the generous loan of very rare source materials; to Panos P. Morphos, Catherine Savage Brosman, Harry Redman, Jr., Giovanni Cecchetti, and the members of the Editorial Committee of the *TSRLL* for their invaluable suggestions and criticism; and to Mrs. Sid Dupois, Jane Reece, and Mary Ann Brasted for their gracious help in the preparation of the manuscript. Parts of the introduction and conclusion were included in an article entitled *"Ubu Roi* and the New Comedy" which appeared in the *New Orleans Review,* Vol. 3, No. 1 (1972). My thanks also go to the editors for their permission to reprint this material.

INTRODUCTION

The first performance of *Ubu Roi* took place to the accompaniment of violent jeers and hurrahs on the night of December 10, 1896, at the Théâtre de l'Œuvre in Paris. The author, Alfred-Henri Jarry, who was then barely twenty-three years old, was as yet completely unknown outside of a few literary circles. Nevertheless, the performance was a theatrical event of such magnitude that it has often been compared to the violent "bataille d'Hernani" which marked the beginning of the Romantic theater.

Before the curtain rose, Jarry, who resembled an overgrown marionette, marched solemnly on stage, sat down at a crude table covered with a piece of sack cloth and read, in a monotone voice that matched his dead-pan face, a very enigmatic speech. After first thanking the critics who had already spoken favorably of the play and then describing Ubu in terms of a complex pseudo-scientific metaphor in which he compared him to a sphere, Jarry continued in the following vein:

Il a plu à quelques acteurs de se faire pour deux soirées impersonnels et de jouer enfermés dans un masque, afin d'être bien exactement l'homme intérieur et l'âme des grandes marionnettes que vous allez voir. La pièce ayant été montée hâtivement et surtout avec un peu de bonne volonté, Ubu n'a pas eu le temps d'avoir son masque véritable, d'ailleurs très incommode à porter, et ses comparses seront comme lui décorés plutôt d'approximations....

Nous aurons d'ailleurs un décor parfaitement exact, car de même qu'il est un procédé facile pour situer une pièce dans l'Eternité, à savoir de faire par exemple tirer en l'an mille et tant des coups de revolver, vous verrez des portes s'ouvrir sur des plaines de neige sous un ciel bleu, des cheminées garnies de pendules se fendre afin de servir de portes, et des palmiers verdir au pied des lits, pour que les broutent de petits éléphants perchés sur des étagères.

Quant à notre orchestre qui manque, on n'en regrettera que l'intensité et le timbre, divers pianos et timbales exécutant les thèmes d'Ubu derrière la coulisse.

Quant à l'action, qui va commencer, elle se passe en Pologne, c'est-à-dire Nulle Part. [1]

Jarry retreated, the table was removed, and the curtain rose to reveal a set painted by Jarry himself with the assistance of such artists as Pierre Bonnard, Vuillard, Toulouse-Lautrec, and Serusier. Arthur Symons, who was present at the turbulent *première*, gives a detailed description of the scenery in his *Studies in Seven Arts*:

... the scenery was painted to represent, by a child's conventions, indoors and out of doors, and even the torrid, temperate and arctic zones at once. Opposite to you, at the back of the stage, you saw apple-trees in bloom, under a blue sky, and against the sky a small closed window and a fireplace containing an alchemist's crucible through the very midst of which trooped in and out these clamorous and sanguinary persons of the drama. On the left was painted a bed, and at the foot of the bed a bare tree, and snow falling. On the right there were palm trees about one of which coiled a boa-constrictor; a door opened against the sky, and beside the door a skeleton dangled from a gallows. [2]

But if the audience had been surprised by the enigmatic speech of the author and the highly stylized decor, their greatest shock was yet to come. Firmin Gemier, who played the part of Ubu, stepped forward and delivered the opening word in a flat, clipped voice suggestive of that of the author himself: "Merdre!" With the pronouncement of the slightly distorted but perfectly recognizable "mot de Cambronne," pandemonium broke out. It was fully fifteen minutes before the audience was quiet enough for the performance to be resumed. And the vociferous interruptions continued throughout the evening with each repetition of the "word." (It occurs thirty-three times in the course of the play.) Here is how William Butler Yeats, who was also present, described his own reactions to this important and tumultuous literary event:

I go to the first performance of Jarry's *Ubu-Roi*, at the Théâtre de l'Œuvre, ... The audience shake their fists at one another, ... The players are supposed to be dolls, toys, marionettes, and now they are all hopping like wooden frogs, and I can see for myself that the chief personage, who is some kind of king carries for a sceptre a brush of the kind that we use to clean a closet. Feeling bound

---

[1] Alfred Jarry, *Tout Ubu* (Paris: Editions Fasquelle, 1968), pp. 19-20.

[2] Arthur Symons, *Studies in Seven Arts* (New York: E. P. Dutton and Company, 1907), pp. 373-374.

to support the most spirited party, we have shouted for the play, but that night at the Hotel Corneille I am very sad, for comedy, objectivity, has displayed its growing power once more. I say, after S. Mallarmé, after Verlaine, after G. Moreau, after Puvis de Chavannes, after our own verse, after the faintest mixed hints of Condor, what more is possible? After us the Savage God. [3]

It is understandable that the audience should have reacted violently to *Ubu Roi* since the play presented a new form of comedy for which there were no immediate literary precedents. Ubu appeared on the scene at a time when the theater was dominated by the realistic and naturalistic schools of drama brought in vogue by Antoine and the Théâtre Libre. In contrast to the prevailing tradition, *Ubu Roi* is entirely antirealistic in every aspect — plot, character, language, and mise-en-scène.

If the scenery of *Ubu Roi,* described by Arthur Symons, evokes visions of a child's bedroom, the action of the play itself suggests nothing so much as the nightmare fantasy of an extremely intelligent and precocious child. Ubu, who is a greedy, vulgar officer in the Polish King's army, assassinates the king, usurps the throne, kills a number of people, pillages the countryside, and is finally defeated by the fourteen-year-old prince and his supporters. It is obviously the parody of a traditional plot of high adventure or tragedy. Parody is also present in the individual episodes which are equally traditional in such a plot. They include a conspirator's dinner, a military review at which the assassination takes place, a purge of the former supporters of the king, two battles, a fight with a bear in a cave, a dream sequence, and finally, a voyage by water.

The characters reveal the same exaggerated simplicity as that of the basic plot. In fact, they are essentially overgrown marionettes and as such also seem to have come from the world of children. The cast includes such universal types as the good but gullible king, the bereaved queen, the young prince who must avenge his father, the undeserving usurper of the throne, his ambitious wife, and the conspirator who later repents and helps to bring about the downfall of the usurper.

As the title indicates, the play is dominated by the monstrous and grotesque figure of le Père Ubu himself. In Ubu, Jarry has created a new comic type. Ubu's most conspicuous characteristic, his belly, is the physical manifestation or symbol of his entire inner nature. Jarry ex-

---

[3] William Butler Yeats, *Autobiographies* (London: Macmillan, 1955), pp. 348-349.

plained in his "Paralipomènes d'Ubu" which was published in the *Revue Blanche* on December 1, 1896, immediately preceding the first performance of the play: "Des trois âmes que distingue Platon: de la tête, du cœur et de la gidouille, cette dernière seule, en lui, n'est pas embryonnaire." [4] Ubu, then, is the embodiment of the basest human instincts. He is a total glutton — for food, riches, power — and an ingrate. He is a complete coward and, at the same time, a sadist. Above all, he is overwhelmingly obscene. As Catulle Mendès so aptly put it, Ubu is the incarnation "de l'éternelle imbécilité humaine, de l'éternelle luxure, de l'éternelle goinfrerie, de la bassesse de l'instinct érigée en tyrannie; des pudeurs, des vertus, du patriotisme, et de l'idéal des gens qui ont bien dîné." [5] Ubu's evil is unrelieved by any redeeming characteristic. He is more than just unaware of his own evil, he seems actually to enjoy it.

Ubu not only overshadows the other characters in the play, he and "la Mère Ubu," who is merely his other half, "Madame ma moitié" as Ubu himself calls her, also monopolize the dialogue. The style, then, is intimately linked to the character of Ubu, to the point that it has been dubbed "le parler Ubu" in Parisian literary circles. It presents a unique combination of seemingly disparate elements: vulgarity and fanciful invention, pomposity and colloquialism, a limited but piquant vocabulary, and a sophisticated use of rhetorical patterns. The style employs many of the traditional techniques of the burlesque. And its free invention of language both harks back to the medieval theater and looks forward to the linguistic ingenuity of Ionesco and other contemporary avant-garde dramatists.

The manner of staging the play also presented a unique combination of new and old techniques. As Jarry mentioned in his Preliminary Address to the audience, the actors were supposed to represent marionettes. There was a single decor and the methods of indicating changes of scene were also borrowed from the marionette theater. Much of the slapstick that is found in the play can also be traced back to "guignolesque" techniques of comedy. In fact, the principles of the marionette theater formed the basis for Jarry's dramatic theories which were in revolt against the popular dramatic conventions of his day. These theories were first and perhaps most clearly expressed in a letter to Lugné-Poe, director of the

---

[4] In *Tout Ubu*, p. 151.
[5] In Alfred Jarry, "Questions de théâtre," *Tout Ubu*, p. 140.

Théâtre de l'Œuvre, in which Jarry offered Ubu for presentation and made specific suggestions as to the manner in which it should be staged. [6] In later articles, Jarry returned again and again to the "supériorité suggestive" of the marionette theater with its universal characters and gestures, preferable to the more superficial realism and naturalism of the day. His ideas planted the seeds for a complete renovation in the modern theater.

There were only two performances of *Ubu Roi* at the Théâtre de l'Œuvre, but Jarry became the most controversial figure on the literary scene. For several weeks after the first performance, the critics engaged in a verbal battle over *Ubu Roi* in the newspapers. The five critics whom Jarry mentioned in his Preliminary Address wrote enthusiastically favorable reviews but a dozen others sided with Francisque Sarcey of *Le Temps,* who sanctimoniously called the play "une fumisterie ordurière qui ne mérite que le silence du mépris" [7] and treated it as a grotesque and childish hoax. The battle narrowed to a verbal duel between Henry Bauer of the *Echo de Paris* who defended *Ubu* and Henry Fouquier of the more conservative *Le Figaro* who attacked it.

Bauer had already stated his position in an article that appeared in the *Echo de Paris* before the actual performance of the play:

C'est une farce extraordinaire, de verbe excessif, de grossièreté énorme, de la truculente fantaisie recouvrant la verve mordante et aggressive, débordant de l'altier mépris des hommes et des choses; c'est un pamphlet philosophico-politique à gueule effrontée, qui crache au visage des chimères de la tradition et des maîtres inventés, selon les respects des peuples: c'est une contribution aux Faits et Gestes de Gargantua et de son fils Pantagruel. C'est enfin ce qui s'entend de plus rare, un cri original et discord dans le concert des accoutumances. Et ce cri résonne longuement et admirablement aux oreilles qui l'écoutèrent. . . . [8]

He continued his wholehearted support of the play in articles appearing in the same paper on the twelfth and nineteenth of December.

But for Fouquier, *Ubu Roi* presented an ill wind that was blowing through the Parisian theatrical scene and, while pretending to support the avant-garde movement, he warned the public in solemn tones not to take such "fumisteries" seriously. He concluded in these words:

---

[6] See *Tout Ubu,* pp. 123-124.

[7] Quoted in *Cahiers du College de 'Pataphysique,* No. 3-4 (1951), 75.

[8] Quoted in Charles Chassé, *Dans les coulisses de la gloire, d'Ubu-Roi au Douanier Rousseau* (Paris: Editions de la Nouvelle Critique, n. d.), p. 13.

Tout ami sincère du progrès en toutes choses est tenu de le défendre contre ceux qui le perdent et font des réactionnaires par la violence de leurs sottises. Hier, au théâtre de l'Œuvre, un spectateur a crié "Vive feu Monsieur Scribe!" Comprendra-t-on la leçon? J'espère que oui: et la soirée d'*Ubu-Roi* me paraît avoir une importance symptomatique considérable. En quoi elle me semble être excellente, victoire du bon sens éclairé et progressiste sur la niaiserie grossière et de l'art véritable sur la caricature de l'art. [9]

Fouquier won the duel and Bauer lost his position on the *Echo de Paris*; but Jarry, and Ubu, won the war. What Fouquier seemed to forget is that the critic cannot impose his own taste on the artist and, in fact, not even on the public whom he supposedly serves. Perhaps, then, the reactions of other writers and "hommes de théâtre" who were present at that first performance can afford a better measure of the impact of *Ubu Roi* on the theatrical and literary world. We have already seen that William Butler Yeats, who could not even understand French, was obviously aware of the importance of the event. As Marcel Schwob, to whom the published edition of the play was dedicated, said to Rachilde during the performance: "Il est un signe des temps." [10] And Mallarmé wrote to Jarry after the performance:

Vous avez mis, debout avec une glaise rare et durable au doigt, un personnage prodigieux et les siens, cela, en sobre et sûr sculpteur dramatique. Il entre dans le répertoire de haut goût et me hante. [11]

Jacques Copeau, who was at the time a young man of seventeen, wrote later about the performance:

Qu'on lui attribue le sens que l'on voudra, *Ubu-Roi* de Jarry c'est du théâtre *cent pour cent,* comme nous dirions aujourd'hui, du théâtre pur, synthétique, poussant jusqu'au scandale l'usage avoué de la convention, créant, en marge du réel, une réalité avec des signes. [12]

In spite of occasional eclipses, the figure of Ubu has continued to hover over the literary and theatrical scene ever since, and never so sig-

---

[9] In *Cahiers du Collège de 'Pataphysique*, No. 3-4 (1951), 85.

[10] Quoted in Rachilde, "Roman: les Jours et les Nuits," *Mercure de France*, 23 (July, 1897), 143.

[11] Undated letter to Jarry, quoted in Stéphane Mallarmé, *Propos sur la Poésie*, ed. H. Mondor (Monaco: Editions du Rocher, 1953), p. 195.

[12] Jacques Copeau, *L'Art du théâtre* (Montréal: Editions Serge, 1944), p. 149.

nificantly as today. His shadow was clearly visible in the experimental plays of Apollinaire and Cocteau. And the Surrealists and Dadaists openly admitted their debt to him.

Jarry's influence on the entire modern theater and especially on the recent theater of the avant-garde in France was crystallized when Antonin Artaud founded the Théâtre Alfred Jarry in 1927 for the express purpose of bringing about the theatrical revolution that Jarry had called for in 1896. Artaud took the essence of Jarry's vision of the world and of his random remarks on the theater and formulated from them a complete theatrical philosophy, published in 1938 under the title *Le Théâtre et son double,* which has become the basic manifesto for the contemporary avant-garde movement.

It is not difficult to understand that Jarry's sardonic vision of the world has attained increasing significance in a century in which man's powers of destruction have far outstripped his ability to control them and in which his mastery of technique has overshadowed his understanding of himself and of the increasingly complex world in which he lives. Cyril Connolly was indeed right when he dubbed Ubu the "Santa Claus of the Atomic Age." [13] As Roger Shattuck has said:

We are all Ubu, still blissfully ignorant of our destructiveness and systematically practicing the soul-devouring "reversal" of flushing our conscience down the john. Ubu, unruffled king of tyrants and cuckolds, is more terrifying than tragedy. [14]

In the absurd world of the twentieth century, comedy seems quite appropriate as an artistic reflection of our feelings of bewilderment and helplessness in a chaotic world we cannot comprehend. And consequently, laughter becomes a means for catharsis. Jarry himself once said to a friend and collaborator, Dr. Jean Saltas:

Raconter des choses compréhensibles ne sert qu'à alourdir l'esprit et fausser la mémoire tandis que l'absurde exerce l'esprit et fait travailler la mémoire. [15]

Humor, then, for Jarry was a very serious business. And he was the first of the moderns to understand that the more elemental and violent the humor, the greater the catharsis it produced.

---

[13] *Ideas and Places* (New York: Harper and Bros., 1953), pp. 38-39.

[14] Introduction to *Selected Works* of Alfred Jarry, ed. by Roger Shattuck and Simon Watson Taylor (New York: Grove Press, 1965), p. 10.

[15] Quoted in Pronko, *op. cit.*, p. 17.

I

HISTORICAL BACKGROUND

As Jarry himself stated in his Preliminary Address at the Théâtre de l'Œuvre, [1] the character of Ubu was actually based on a living model. In fact, the entire play grew out of a series of schoolboy satires invented by Jarry and his classmates at the Lycée de Rennes against a certain physics professor named Monsieur Hébert. Here is how another student from Rennes, Paul Chauveau, describes Professor Hébert:

> Or, ces qualités (bonté, intelligence et supériorité) manquaient totalement à M. Hébert, professeur de physique ... c'était un gros homme court, de chair épaisse et blafarde, de poil rare. Le visage était porcin, les yeux petits. Il était tout plein de dignité grotesque et de triste colère maladroite, le malheureux avait de pauvres filles épaisses comme lui et qui lui ressemblaient, si bien qu'on les nommait "cochonnettes." Cette affreuse famille aimait le monde et ne manquait pas une seule occasion de se faire inviter. M. Hébert, économe et gourmand, remplissait, dit-on, chaque fois qu'il le pouvait, ses poches de bonbons, de petits fours et de gâteaux. [2]

Professor Hébert, "Père Heb" or simply "le P. H." as the students called him, was the butt of many practical jokes and the subject of innumerable satires and mock-epics invented by the abundant imagination of the young lycéens, even before Jarry entered the school. Again, according to Monsieur Chauveau,

---

[1] See *Tout Ubu*, p. 19.
[2] "Notes sur Alfred Jarry," *Mercure de France*, 191, No. 681 (November 1, 1926), 589-590.

Il y eut, à cette époque, au lycée de Rennes, un véritable cycle de rapsodies à base de fous rires, tantôt étouffés, tantôt éclatants, sur le personnage héroïque du P. H. Ces jeunes garçons retrouvent naturellement la manière et l'abondance des épopées primitives qu'on a parfois cru l'œuvre d'une inspiration collective. Les textes concernant le père Hébert furent innombrables, parlés ou transcrits sur des feuilles volantes, pour la plupart éphemères. [3]

The boys imitated or burlesqued everything they read in or out of class. Among their models figured some of the greatest names in literature: Rabelais, Cervantes, Shakespeare, and others.

Charles Morin, another student at the lycée who was involved in the *cycle ubique* and who later claimed to be the principal author of *Ubu Roi*, [4] has given an example of the origin and characteristics of P. H. according to the oral tradition:

... Sous le règne de M. Dromberg III naquit, sur les bords de l'Oxus, le P. H., résultat du commerce d'un Homme-Zénorme avec une sorcière tartare ou mongole qui vivait dans les joncs et les roseaux des rives de la mer d'Aral.

Caractéristiques du P. H.—Il naquit avec son chapeau forme simili-cronstadt, sa robe de laine et son pantalon à carreaux. Il porte sur le haut de la tête une seule oreille extensible qui, en temps normal, est ramassée sous son chapeau; il a les deux bras du même côté (comme ont les yeux des soles) et, au lieu d'avoir les pieds, un de chaque bord comme les humains, les a, dans le prolongement l'un de l'autre, de sorte que quand il vient à tomber, il ne peut pas se ramasser tout seul et reste à gueuler sur place jusqu'à ce qu'on vienne le ramasser. Il n'a que trois dents, une dent de pierre, une de fer et une de bois. Quand ses dents de la mâchoire supérieure commencent à percer, il se les renfonce à coups de pied. . . . [5]

At one point in his long and varied career, Père Heb is turned into a fish and swims up the Seine to Paris where he is pulled out of the water by a fisherman. As he comes out of the water, Père Heb assumes his original form which is so horrible that the unfortunate fisherman flees terrified. "Puis, ce fut le voyage en Espagne, l'usurpation du royaume d'Aragon, le départ en Pologne comme capitaine de dragons, etc. . . . , etc." [6] The etceteras refer to the action of *Ubu Roi*.

---

[3] Chauveau, *Alfred Jarry*, pp. 40-41.
[4] See below, p. 32 ff.
[5] Quoted in Chassé, *D'Ubu-Roi au Douanier Rousseau*, p. 28.
[6] Quoted *ibid.*, p. 32.

Although the Hébert legends were in existence before Jarry entered the Lycée de Rennes in October, 1888, he immediately became one of the major collaborators on the cycle of epics and plays. And it was Jarry who initiated and promoted the idea of actually staging the plays, especially one entitled *Les Polonais* which was an early version of *Ubu Roi*. Henri Morin, younger brother of Charles who also became involved in the dispute over the authorship of *Ubu Roi,* but who was at that time a close friend of Jarry and a major contributor to the *cycle ubique,* has given an account of their productions of the plays:

... Jarry ... me suggéra l'idée de mettre la pièce à la scène. La chose était facile. Nous habitions à cette époque une grande maison ... dont les combles immenses se prêtaient admirablement à l'installation d'un théâtre d'amateurs. Jarry, fort artiste, eut vite fait de brosser les décors, et les acteurs (ainsi que le public) se trouvèrent aisément parmi nos camarades de classe. C'est en décembre 1888 ou janvier 1889 que fut donné la première représentation et il y en eut de nombreuses, au grand détriment de nos versions latines et de nos auteurs grecs. [7]

They also staged *Les Polonais* with marionettes which they fabricated themselves. Again to cite Henri Morin:

Elles [les marionnettes] furent confectionnées par nous sur le modèle des personnages des *Polonais*. Mlle Jarry, un peu plus âgée que son frère, collabora activement à cette œuvre. Je me souviens, en particulier, d'un czar Alexis sorti de ses mains et qui était du plus haut cocasse avec son bonnet à poils et sa tête de diable sortant d'une boîte. A l'usage, le maniement des marionnettes nous parut trop compliqué et c'est alors que nous passâmes au théâtre d'ombres. [8]

Mademoiselle Jarry also made an excellent sculpture of Père Heb, according to Charles Morin's oral testimony to Chassé:

Elle sculpta dans la glaise un magnifique buste du P. H., gidouille comprise. Comme le P. H. était son voisin et qu'il passait tous les jours sous sa fenêtre, elle put remettre très souvent le buste au point et parvint ainsi à une ressemblance absolue. [9]

It has been conjectured that there was even a musical accompaniment to the plays with Madame Jarry, Alfred's mother, at the piano.

---

[7] Quoted *ibid.,* p. 44.
[8] Quoted *ibid.,* p. 45.
[9] Quoted *ibid.,* p. 49.

During this same period, i.e. the years 1888-1889, a second *cycle ubique* which would eventually become the play *Ubu Cocu* was elaborated at Rennes by Jarry and Henri Morin. There seem to have been several different plays or versions of this second cycle. A fragment of one version dating from 1888 or 1889 entitled *Onésime ou les tribulations de Priou* has been preserved and published in the *Cahiers du Collège de 'Pataphysique*. [10] The main character of this play, besides le P. H. and la Mère Eb., is the title character, Onésime O'Priou, "futur ??? bachelier." The action of the play is purely episodic with little or no connection between the various incidents. For example, the action jumps abruptly from a monastery to the laboratory of P. H., [11] to a shoe shop, and elsewhere. The main episode is based on a rather gratuitous accident. It is night; Onésime, drunk on wine he has stolen from the monastery, stumbles onto the house of P. H. and rings the doorbell for no apparent reason. Mère Eb., thinking it is her lover, calls out to him from a second story window: "Est-ce toi, mon cher Barbapoux?" Onésime, in his drunken stupor, thinks she is calling to him and says:

Priou (*à part*).

J'ai entendu parler: ouou, Priou, ouou, je n'entends que ça. Je crois que c'est à moi que s'adresse cette jeune personne. On se croirait viâ Poulariaria. Au fait, avec un physique comme le mien, on peut s'attendre à tout. Je serai bientôt obligé de rester dans un tube fermé à la lampe, sous une couche d'huile, pour ne pas troubler toute la population féminine de l'univers. (*Haut.*)

Mais oui, me voilà à vos pieds. Déscendez-moi un escalier par la fenêtre, et je monterai vers vous; là, vous offrant mon cœur sur un plat d'argent, je pourrai vous dire qu'il vous est offert par la main des Grâces? (*A part.*) Suis-je galant, ce soir?

Onésime then begins to climb up toward Mère Eb. but is caught in the act by P. H. who has been warned by one of his strange henchmen, the Palotins, that he would be made a cuckold by Onésime at that particular moment, "la 25e heure sidérale." The Palotins throw Onésime to the ground and P. H. threatens him with extreme and bizarre tortures:

---

[10] *Cahier*, No. 20 (1955). See also *Tout Ubu*, pp. 161-181. All quotations are taken from the latter edition.

[11] This is obviously a reminiscence of the physics laboratory of Professor Hébert. "La 'Pataphysique," a science invented by Ubu, plays an important role in this second *cycle ubique*.

... Il n'y a rien à faire de Priou. On se contentera de lui faire torsion du nez et des oneilles [sic], avec supplices successifs:

du pal simple,
du pal grave,
du pal de la compagnie du gaz,
du pal azotique,
du pal détonnant (simplicité bon goût);

Puis deuxième édition de la torsion du nez et des oneilles, comme ci-dessus, et finalement découpage en 98 000 petits copeaux, avec la machine à découper brevetée SGDG, en 6 jours, avec une sage lenteur. Ensuite, Priou sera, de par notre mansuétude, libre d'aller se faire pendre ailleurs: il ne lui sera pas fait d'autre mal, car je le veux bien traiter.

It is obvious from these examples that the humor in this play is quite primitive and reflects the age and mentality of the authors. Another typical illustration of this adolescent humor is the "scène du savetier." Onésime goes to a shoemaker's shop to get some shoes and the shoemaker lists his wares as follows:

... J'ai les Ecrase-Merdres. Il y en a pour tous les goûts. Voici pour la merdre récente. Voici pour le crottin de cheval. Voici pour la merdre ancienne. Voici pour la bouse de vache. Voici pour les gogs ordinaires. Voici pour la merdre de gendarme.

The Palotins appear and a burlesque fight ensues in which one character is thrown into a tub of water, another sits on a nail, and the shop is completely destroyed. The slapstick, the violence, the scatology, and the verbal fantasy were all traditional characteristics of the Ubu cycles composed at the Lycée de Rennes. Jarry was later able in reworking *Les Polonais* into *Ubu Roi* to handle these same elements with great skill and art while deliberately retaining the primitive flavor and earthy humor of the schoolboy tradition.

There seem to have been other versions or plays that were part of this same cycle. Henri Morin speaks of a play in which the principal characters, besides le P. H., were

deux universitaires rennais, M. B*** et M. P*** et aussi le bel Octave. M. Pr..., alors élève du lycée. La pièce roulait tout entière sur une rivalité amoureuse, toute fictive, qui aurait mis aux prises M. Pr... et M. B*** lesquels désiraient tous deux épouser la fille du P. H. [12]

---

[12] Quoted in Chassé, *op. cit.*, p. 70.

Polyhedra, which appear in *Ubu Cocu,* also played a major role in this early work, according to M. Morin. In his article "Les Paralipomènes d'Ubu," Jarry himself speaks of another play in this cycle:

Une pièce ancienne l'a glorifié (*Les Cornes du P. U.,* où Madame Ubu accouche d'un archéoptéryx), qui a été jouée en ombres, et dont la scène est l'intérieur de [la] gidouille [d'Ubu]. [13]

When questioned about this play, Henri Morin did not remember collaborating on it:

Je ne me souviens pas des *Cornes du Père Ubu* dont a parlé Jarry. Il s'agit sans doute d'une fantaisie composée par lui à Paris et jouée peut-être sur le théâtre d'ombres qu'il avait alors installé dans leur logement du boulevard de Port Royal. Cette pièce fut peut-être inspirée d'une de celles qui précédèrent *Les Polonais* et qui était intitulée les *Andouilles du Père Ubu.* [14]

In another letter to Monsieur Chassé, Morin adds that part of the action of the *Andouilles du Père Ubu* took place inside Ubu's enormous *gidouille* where the Palotins were performing a "nettoyage interne" necessitated by the fact that Ubu had, as usual, consumed too many *andouilles.* If *Les Cornes du P. U.* did exist, it has not survived, but there are fragments of another version of this cycle entitled *Ubu Cocu ou l'Archéoptéryx* [15] in which one act does take place inside Ubu's *gidouille* and the action is similar to that described by Henri Morin.

Jarry remained three years at the Lycée de Rennes and received his Baccalaureat in 1891. That same year he left for Paris with the intention of preparing for the Ecole Normale Supérieure at the Lycée Henri IV. But he did not forget Père Hébert. Soon he gave up the idea of the Ecole

---

[13] In *Tout Ubu,* p. 151.

[14] Quoted in Chassé, *op. cit.,* p. 46.

[15] These fragments were originally published in the *Cahiers du Collège de 'Pataphysique,* Nos. 3-4 and 26-27. They also appear in *Tout Ubu,* pp. 227-244. According to J. Hughes Sainmont, whose article entitled "Occultations et Exaltations d'Ubu Cocu," accompanied the original publication of these fragments (see *Cahiers du Collège,* No. 3-4, pp. 29-36), this version of the play was not composed until later, i.e. circa 1897, and therefore after the publication of several sections of *Les Polyèdres.* Certain similarities between the fragments of this play and those of *Onésime* might lead one to suspect, however, that this play was an intermediate version that preceded *Les Polyèdres* or *Ubu Cocu* and was possibly composed between 1891 and 1893.

Normale and decided to attempt a literary career. Père Hébert, rechristened Père Ubu, played an important role from the very beginning. In his small apartment on the Boulevard de Port Royal, Jarry did install a *théâtre d'ombres* and gave shadow plays for his new friends, among them another young man with literary ambitions, Léon-Paul Fargue. Naturally, the material was drawn from the various Ubu cycles on which Jarry had been a collaborator at the Lycée de Rennes.

Soon Jarry began to make important literary contacts with, among others, Catulle Mendès and Marcel Schwob, editors of *L'Echo de Paris littéraire illustré,* and then Alfred Vallette, editor of the *Mercure de France,* and his wife, Madame Rachilde, novelist and critic. Vallette and Rachilde held regular receptions at the offices of the *Mercure* on Tuesday afternoons and they welcomed Jarry into their circle. Among the frequent guests at these receptions were the most noted figures of the Symbolist Movement: Rémy de Gourmont, [16] Henri de Régnier, Albert Samain, Pierre Louys, Gustave Kahn, Charles-Henri Hirsch, Franc-Nohain, and others. Younger, less well-known figures, like Jarry, were Valéry and Gide. Because of his outlandish dress and behavior, Jarry became one of the favorites of the group. Soon, i.e. probably toward the end of 1893 and the beginning of 1894, he was entertaining them with readings of passages from *Ubu Roi,* as *Les Polonais* was now called. Jean de Tinan, another regular member of the *Mercure* group, recalls these readings in a letter written to Jarry in 1896:

J'ai relu hier le *drame* en son intégrité (avec pas mal de petits changements, et très heureux, m'a-t-il semblé). Il m'a semblé vous l'entendre lire une fois de plus — avec accompagnement du rire de Rachilde, du rire de Moréno, du rire de Fanny, du rire de Vallette, du rire de Schwob, du rire de Herold et du rire de tout le monde. [17]

Ubu's audience was growing ever wider.

Ubu made his first appearance in print as early as April 28, 1893, in *L'Echo de Paris littéraire illustré.* Significantly, the title of the selection was "Guignol." It consisted of three sections, two of which contained

---

[16] Jarry and Gourmont founded and directed together a short-lived art review called *L'Ymagier* in 1894. After their rupture in 1896, *L'Ymagier* ended, but Jarry began another review, *Perhinderion,* that lasted only two issues.

[17] Quoted in *Tout Ubu,* p. 11.

scenes taken from the play *Ubu Cocu,* then entitled *Les Polyèdres.* The first section, entitled "L'Autoclète" (in Greek, "he who invites himself"), included the first four scenes of *Les Polyèdres,* and the third section, entitled "L'Art et la Science," included most of the fourth act of the play. "Guignol" won a prize for the best prose work by a young author and also became part of Jarry's first book, *Les Minutes de Sable Mémorial,* which was published by the Editions du Mercure de France in October, 1894.

Ubu Roi did not see the light of day until a year later. It too first appeared in an abbreviated form as part of another work, i.e., as the third act, "L'Acte terrestre," of *César-Antéchrist,* a quasi-mystical, quasi-blasphemous work that combines extremes of subject matter and style. The first act, "L'Acte prologal," had appeared in *L'Art Littéraire* in July-August, 1894. "L'Acte héraldique" was published in the *Mercure de France* in March, 1895, and "L'Acte terrestre" appeared in the *Mercure* in September, 1895. "L'Acte terrestre" contains the following parts of *Ubu Roi*: I, vi, vii; II, i, ii, vi; III, i-vii, viii (with minor variations); IV, iii-vii. The entire work, *César-Antéchrist,* appeared in book form in October, 1895, in the Editions du Mercure de France.

Jarry's friends to whom he had read the play also encouraged him to try to produce it. By a stroke of good fortune, he was soon invited by Lugné-Poe to become *secrétaire-régisseur* of the Théâtre de l'Œuvre, the most avant-garde theatrical group in Paris at the time. Jarry offered both *Les Polyèdres* and *Ubu Roi* for presentation. Here is how Lugné-Poe later recalls his reactions to the plays in a book of memoirs:

Il me remit, puis il me retira un essai schématique d'imagination poétique: *les Polyèdres.* Auparavant, il m'avait communiqué non achevé *Ubu Roi,* que je ne savais par quel bout prendre pour le réaliser à la scène. [18]

However, Jarry, who had not forgotten his experiences with marionettes in the attic at Rennes, realized that there was only one suitable way to stage *Ubu Roi,* and that was *en guignol.* In January, 1896, Jarry wrote a long letter to Lugné-Poe, [19] which was later published as a preface to the play, giving his ideas and recommendations on the matter.

---

[18] Lugné-Poe, *Parade: Acrobaties* (Paris: Gallimard, 1931), p. 160.

[19] See below, pp. 52, 106. For the complete text of the letter, see *Tout Ubu,* pp. 123-124.

The year 1896 was undoubtedly the most important year in the literary career of both Jarry and *Ubu*. In April and May the complete play, *Ubu Roi ou les Polonais*, appeared in two installments in Paul Fort's *Le Livre d'Art*. It was then published in book form by the Editions du Mercure de France on June 11. The subtitle expressed Jarry's debt to the schoolboy experiments in Rennes: "Drame en cinq actes en prose/ Restitué en son intégrité/ tel qu'il a été représenté par/ les Marionnettes du Théâtre des Phynances en 1888." On December 10, 1896, eight years later, *Ubu Roi* finally received its first performance. From that day on, Alfred Jarry and *Ubu* were famous.

A few days before the performance of *Ubu Roi*, Jarry published an article in *La Revue Blanche* entitled "Les Paralipomènes d'Ubu" which contained other fragments of *Les Polyèdres*. They include II, ii, iii; III, iii, iv; and V, i, iii, iv. Except for a few differences in names, the scenes are identical with those of the published edition of *Ubu Cocu*. Since most of Acts I and IV had been included in "Guignol," one can see that a large part of the play was already in print.

In October, 1897, the Editions du Mercure de France published an "édition fac-similé autographique" of *Ubu Roi* that included the music which Claude Terrasse had composed for the original production of the play.

Approximately one year later, in January, 1898, *Ubu Roi* was performed by marionettes at the Théâtre des Pantins, 6 rue Ballu, which was in actuality the studio of Claude Terrasse who was at the piano and who had composed several new pieces for this production. The marionettes belonged to Pierre Bonnard. Louise France, the original Mère Ubu, was the voice of Mère Ubu. Other participants included Fanny Zaessinger, Jovita Nadal, Jacotot, and Lardennoy. One member of the audience later reported that Jarry himself was the voice of Père Ubu. [20] The audiences at these performances were necessarily limited by the small size of the theater and were made up largely of literati and friends of Jarry. This production *en famille* was probably the most authentic

---

[20] See Maurice Boissard, "Chronique Dramatique: Théâtre de l'Œuvre: *Ubu Roi* d'Alfred Jarry," *Nouvelle Revue Française*, 18, No. 104 (January-June, 1922), 593.

the play has ever received, and it captured better than others the spirit in which the play was written.

In 1899, Jarry wrote a third Ubu play entitled *Ubu enchaîné* as a *contre-partie* of *Ubu Roi*. Ubu has decided to mend his wicked ways and to become a slave. However, his ideas of servitude are just as unusual as his ideas of kingship. He forces his services on a young lady and her uncle, who has the unusual name of Pissembock, and completely disrupts the household until he is thrown in prison and finally condemned to be a galley slave. He accepts his fate with great equanimity, however, and looks forward to new adventures in new lands. One particularly effective scene in this play presents "les Trois Hommes libres" and their corporal who gives them commands which they automatically disobey in order to prove that they are free men. Their motto is "L'indiscipline aveugle et de tous les instants fait la force principale des hommes libres" (I, ii). [21] *Ubu enchaîné,* with *Ubu Roi,* was published in 1900 by the Editions de la Revue Blanche.

The following year, a shortened version of *Ubu Roi* entitled *Ubu sur la Butte* was presented at the Quat'Z'Arts, a cabaret in Montmartre, by the marionettes of the Théâtre Guignol des Gueules de Bois with the participation of Anatole from the Guignol des Champs-Elysées. This was the last performance of any of the Ubu plays during Jarry's lifetime. *Ubu sur la Butte* was not published until five years later in 1906 by Sansot in a collection entitled "Théâtre Mirlitonesque." It was supposed to be followed by the publication of a play entitled *Ubu intime,* one of the versions of *Ubu Cocu,* which never appeared.

On November 1, 1907, Alfred Jarry died at the age of 34. He had left an indelible imprint on the theater. In March, 1908, six months after Jarry's death, *Ubu* was revived at the Théâtre Antoine with somewhat more success than the original production. Firmin Gémier re-created the title role. Thereafter, *Ubu* fell into oblivion for several years.

It was not until 1921, fourteen years after Jarry's death, that there was a revival of interest in *Ubu Roi* which resulted in a second major critical battle over the play. It was occasioned by the publication in November or December of 1921 of a pamphlet entitled *Sous le Masque d'Alfred Jarry? les Sources d'Ubu Roi* in which Charles Chassé contested

---

[21] In *Tout Ubu,* p. 254.

Jarry's authorship of the play. M. Chassé chose his moment well — the play, out of print since 1900, had been re-edited scarcely a month before by Fasquelle. A lively controversy, similar to the one that had followed the first performance, immediately broke out and was fanned by the unsuccessful revival of *Ubu* at the Théâtre de l'Œuvre early the following year.

Chassé's thesis was that the play *Ubu Roi*, or simply *Les Polonais*, as it was then called, had been completely written by the Morin brothers, Charles and Henri, before Jarry ever arrived at the Lycée de Rennes. In late 1920 or early 1921, M. Chassé went to great lengths to contact and question the two Morins, both of whom had since become career artillery officers. They assured him that they were in effect the true authors of *Ubu Roi* which was the last and most important in a series of plays of the *cycle ubique* that they had composed in collaboration. According to Henri Morin, *Les Polonais* was composed in 1885 at the very latest, i.e., three years before Jarry entered the Lycée de Rennes. The brothers were at that time fourteen and ten years old respectively.

Les Polonais was the only one of these plays to survive because, longer than the others, it had been recorded in a notebook. Here is the testimony of Charles Morin, the elder of the two brothers:

J'ai écrit la pièce d'un bout à l'autre sans ratures et, si je l'ai terminée là où elle s'arrête, c'est qu'il ne me restait plus de place. C'est un cahier que je revois encore, un cahier d'une trentaine de pages. Il m'avait servi à tenir le catalogue d'une collection de fossiles, et lorsque je me décidai d'y noter mes élucubrations, il me fallut biffer, puis encadrer de lignes sinueuses toutes ces indications scolaires, le long desquelles serpente le texte des *Polonais*. [22]

Unfortunately, Charles Morin could not clearly remember what had become of the green notebook after he left Rennes. He told Chassé that he had a vague recollection of sending it back to his brother by the intermediary of a classmate named Boris at the Ecole Polytechnique. However, Chassé also reports that this same Boris had given a manuscript of *Ubu Roi* to Franc-Nohain, a member of the group at the *Mercure de France* and friend of Jarry. Franc-Nohain's own account of the episode, which appeared in the *Echo de Paris*, April 26, 1928, throws some doubt on the authenticity of the manuscript in question:

---

[22] Quoted in Chassé, *op. cit.*, p. 34.

Le fameux manuscrit de Charles Morin, — manuscrit sans ratures, alors que le manuscrit original de Jarry est couvert de surcharges et de corrections, — ce manuscrit n'était qu'une copie d'acteur et rien ne dit d'ailleurs que d'autres copies n'existent pas encore de la main d'autres élèves du lycée. . . .

Cette copie qui, encore une fois, n'avait d'autre importance que d'une copie, me fut donnée par Borie [sic] qui la tenait de Charles Morin; . . . [23]

Franc-Nohain added that this copy of the play had apparently been lost during the war in which he, Boris, and the Morins took part.

Henri Morin, on the other hand, seemed convinced that he had retained possession of the manuscript after his brother's departure from Rennes and had given it to Jarry at the time of their productions of *Les Polonais* in the Jarry attic. Chassé also reports Henri's recollection of the sequence of events:

C'est au commencement de l'été de 1889 que je remis le manuscrit original à Jarry. Depuis cette époque, je ne l'ai plus jamais eu entre les mains . . . D'ailleurs, c'est à Paris, dans le courant de 1893, que Jarry composa l'*Ubu Roi* qui fut joué à l'Œuvre et qui, à part la modification des Hidalgos et quelques autres de même ordre, reproduit identiquement le texte primitif. Jarry n'aurait pu se livrer à ce travail de reconstitution — bien qu'il eût une mémoire extraordinaire — sans avoir le texte sous les yeux . . . [24]

More important than the question of whether or not Jarry had possession of the supposedly original manuscript by the Morin brothers and referred to it in composing *Ubu Roi* is the statement by both Charles and Henri Morin that Jarry made few changes, and none of substance, from the original text of the play. Charles Morin wrote in a letter to Henry Bauer shortly after the first performance of *Ubu Roi*:

M. Ubu existe réellement mais sous les espèces d'un énorme, inoffensif et pacifique bonhomme. Il a fallu l'imagination dévergondée de deux potaches, mon frère et moi, actuellement tous deux officiers d'artillerie, pour en faire le monstre sanguinaire, dépeint dans *Ubu-Roi*. Or, cette pièce, si pièce il y a, est notre œuvre commune et Jarry, camarade de mon frère, l'a publiée après avoir simplement changé les noms de quelques personnages. [25]

---

[23] Quoted in Chauveau, *Alfred Jarry*, p. 237.
[24] Quoted in Chassé, *op. cit.*, pp. 35-36.
[25] Quoted *ibid.*, p. 104.

Since the green notebook was missing, Charles and Henri had corrected, supposedly in 1907 and 1908, a copy of an edition of *Ubu Roi* [26] in order to reestablish the original text of the lost manuscript. In spite of Morin's confusion over what he had done with the green notebook, Chassé professed complete faith in his ability to remember every syllable of the entire play. It is true that the variants given by the Morins are completely insignificant. Here are a few typical examples:

Page 20. "Grande capeline comme celle que j'avais en Aragon et que ces coquins d'Espagnols m'ont impudemment volée." Après le mot: capeline. MM. Charles et Henri M*** ont ajouté: fourée. . . .

Page 21. "Merdre de bougre," rectifié par "de par ma chandelle verte."

Page 28. "Oh! j'ai une idée." Ajouter: lumineuse. "Un balai innomable." Rectifier par "le balai des cabinets."

Page 29. "Cotelettes [sic] de rastron." Rectifier par "côtes de rastron." "Ubu." Rectifier par P. H., comme dans tous les endroits où Jarry a mis "Ubu." . . . [27]

M. Chassé's purpose in attempting to disprove Jarry's authorship of *Ubu Roi* was not simply to restore credit to the rightful authors of the play, i.e., the Morin brothers, but rather was an attempt to discredit the play itself and along with it all the literature of an entire period. Chassé does not hesitate to admit that *Ubu Roi* enjoyed a great deal of success when it appeared in 1896; he even goes so far as to call it "un écrit charactéristique d'une époque, . . . un livre témoin." [28] But then he argues:

S'il apparaissait comme . . . disons: possible qu'*Ubu Roi* fût semblable au nuage d'*Hamlet,* tantôt chameau, belette ou bien monstre marin, suivant l'imagination des regardants, est-ce qu'on ne serait pas tenté de réserver son opinion sur certaines œuvres poétiques de la même époque que l'on persiste à porter au pinnacle, tout en convenant de leur obscurité? [29]

To support his low opinion of the play, Chassé presents the "true" authors' own opinion of the work — which supposedly explains why they

---

[26] M. Chassé calls it the "Perhinderion" edition, which does not exist. However, the original edition published by the *Mercure de France* was printed with the characters of *Perhinderion,* the art review founded and edited by Jarry.

[27] Quoted in Chassé, *op. cit.,* pp. 42-43.

[28] *Ibid.,* p. 11.

[29] *Ibid.,* pp. 10-11.

did not claim authorship of it from the very beginning. Charles Morin's statement on the matter is quite succinct: "Le succès d'*Ubu-Roi*, cela donne la mesure de la bêtise humaine," [30] and when asked why he did not vindicate his paternity of *Ubu Roi*, he replied: "C'est qu'il n'y a pas de quoi être fier quand on a fait une c...nade pareille!" [31] Henri Morin echoed his brother's opinion when in turn he was asked why he did not speak out about the true origins of the play, adding that he and his brother were greatly amused at the spectacle of so many important critics bowing down in adulation before what was nothing more than a school-boy farce.

According to M. Chassé, the success of *Ubu Roi* could be attributed to a strange case of collaboration between author and public. On the one hand, there was at that time a general spirit of social and artistic rebellion and anarchy. Chassé expresses the opinion that in accordance with this spirit, "les spectateurs du moment voulurent . . . voir dans le "Merdre" liminaire du Père Ubu un cri de révolte littéraire et social." [32] On the other hand, there was what he calls the "obscurity" of the play which allowed the spectators to read into it whatever they wished.

In order to dissipate the obscurity of *Ubu Roi* and consequently to destroy its effectiveness, Chassé asked Charles Morin to explain the numerous neologisms and enigmatic expressions that occur throughout the play. First Morin comments on the famous "merdre" that initiated the play with such *éclat*:

Ah! c'est bien simple. N'oubliez pas que nous étions encore des gosses; nos parents ne voulaient naturellement pas que nous fassions usage du mot tel qu'il était, alors, nous avons imaginé d'y intercaler un *r*; voilà tout! [33]

Ubu's oft-used oath "de par ma chandelle verte" came from an earlier play which did not survive. "La chandelle verte était un signal que le P. H. mettait à sa fenêtre pour correspondre avec ses complices, durant les expéditions nocturnes de ceux-ci." [34] The explanation of the origin

---

[30] Quoted *ibid.*, p. 50.

[31] *Ibid.*, pp. 52-53. See, however, Morin's letter to Henri Bauer, quoted above, p. 34.

[32] *Ibid.*, p. 51.

[33] Quoted *ibid.*, p. 40.

[34] Quoted *ibid.*, p. 41.

of the expression "côtelettes de rastron" is perhaps the most interesting of all:

Eh bien! voilà encore quelque chose que les gens ont admiré sans comprendre! Rastron a été mis là tout simplement parce que c'était le surnom de notre camarade Lemaux. Il habitait à Rennes rue de Chapitre. Aussi, nous l'avions surnommé Chapistron, puis chastron, puis le stron; et quelquefois même rastron puisque rat est le contraire de chat. [35]

In concluding his original pamphlet, M. Chassé had summarized his purpose in writing the pamphlet:

Critiques littéraires ... trouveront ici matière, je l'espère, à de savoureuses méditations. Mais ce seront surtout les étudiants de l'époque symboliste qui verront je le crois, surgir nettement tout le danger qu'il peut y avoir à admettre l'obscur comme un élément de beauté littéraire. Car ce que, parfois, on croyait obscur et qu'on admirait comme tel, apparaît très clair et, hélas! ridiculement clair, à partir du moment où on en obtient la clef. Par suite d'un hasard heureux, j'ai pu vider *Ubu-Roi* de toutes les interprétations symboliques que ses lecteurs y avaient mises.... L'important est de savoir si, maintenant que l'outre est vide de tout le vent qui la gonflait, elle pourra, néanmoins, parvenir à rester debout. [36]

As has already been noted, *Ubu Roi,* out of print since 1900, had just been re-edited by Fasquelle in the fall of 1921, only a month or so before the publication of Chassé's pamphlet. A certain amount of critical commentary followed the appearance of this re-edition. Some critics echoed the praise given the play by its most ardent admirers of earlier years. Franc-Nohain wrote in *L'Echo de Paris* on November 3, 1921:

Ubu *existe* et ce n'est pas sans doute sans quelques bonnes raisons; Ubu est et demeure comme une force de la nature; avec sa tête en poire, son vocabulaire spécial et ses tics exaspérés, il apparaît la grimaçante et symbolique figure de toute la bassesse humaine, de tous les vilains appétits, y compris goinfrerie, sottise, vantardise, lâcheté, cruauté, rapacité, hypocrisie et trahison.... [37]

But certain other critics expressed disillusionment with the play. For example, Paul Abram wrote:

---

[35] Quoted *ibid.*
[36] Quoted *ibid.*, p. 56.
[37] Quoted *ibid.*, p. 74.

J'avais admis de confiance qu'*Ubu Roi* était un chef-d'œuvre. Je viens de le lire; quelle déception!... Alors, vraiment, c'était ça, Ubu!... C'était ce fantoche puéril et scatalogique dont on a voulu... enfler le type à l'envergure d'Hamlet, de Tartuffe, de Panurge ou de Don Juan! [38]

The appearance of M. Chassé's pamphlet at the end of 1921 merely increased the critical discussion which was now fragmented onto four or five different points. Certain critics did respond in the way Chassé had intended them to. André Lichtenberger wrote:

Ainsi de la blague de deux écoliers, peu fiers d'une polissonerie qui risquait de leur faire tirer les "oneilles," l'immense jobardisme de notre anarchisme intellec-tuel, aidé par le snobisme du Tout-Paris et la lâcheté de la critique a fait un chef-d'œuvre. [39]

This critic and several others seemed to agree with M. Chassé in his conviction that the success of *Ubu Roi*, proven to be nothing more than a schoolboy farce, revealed the bad taste of an entire literary generation.

As for the defenders of Jarry and *Ubu*, they were divided into several different camps. Some were content to defend Jarry against the accusa-tion of plagiarism. Dr. Jean Saltas, friend and sometime collaborator of Jarry, was quoted as saying: "Jarry était absolument incapable de signer une œuvre qui ne fût pas de lui." [40] And Henri Hirsch, who was among the group at the *Mercure* to whom Jarry had read *Ubu*, came forward with this account:

Vers 1893 ou 1894, quand il nous fit la lecture d'*Ubu Roi*,... le succès de son œuvre auprès de nous lui causa une surprise extrême. Il nous expliqua qu'il avait écrit cela, lycéen, en collaboration avec deux condisciples, pour railler leur pro-fesseur de mathématiques.... Jarry refusa, ce soir-là, de confier son manuscrit à Paul Fort qui publiait alors une revue: *Le Livre d'Art*; telle l'œuvre n'avait pour son auteur aucune valeur littéraire. Il y travailla beaucoup, avant de le donner à l'imprimeur; et nous croyons nous rappeler qu'il s'y décida seulement après avoir consulté Marcel Schwob. [41]

---

[38] In *Comœdia* (November 1, 1921), 1.

[39] "Une bonne blague," *La Victoire*, 6ᵉ année, No. 2160 (December 1, 1921), 1.

[40] Quoted in Pierre de St. Prix, "A la recherche de la paternité d'Ubu. L'Opinion du docteur Jean Saltas," *Ere nouvelle*, 4ᵉ année, No. 749 (January 17, 1922), 3.

[41] "Les Revues," *Mercure de France*, 154 (March 1, 1922), 480.

It is interesting to note that Jarry had never tried to hide the fact that *Ubu* was the result of a collaboration.

Eugène Montfort, editor of *Les Marges*, also maintained in his review of Chassé's book that Jarry played a major role in the creation of *Ubu Roi*, basing his arguments on the style of the play:

M. Chassé qui veut nous persuader que Jarry n'était pour rien dans *Ubu Roi* ne m'a pas convaincu. Ce qui donne de la force à Ubu, c'est plus que l'invention, le style. Ce style-là, certes, aucun collégien ne l'a jamais possédé. Donc, que Jarry ait arrangé une première version d'Ubu courant au lycée de Rennes, cela est fort possible, mais l'arrangement est indéniable et c'est grâce à cet arrangement-là qu'Ubu existe. [42]

Paul Fort, in an article in *Comœdia* on January 8, 1922, defended the Symbolist Movement which had been the real object of Chassé's attack:

Le débat, soulevé par M. Chassé est beaucoup plus important, il ne tend à rien moins qu'à demander la révision de toute l'époque symboliste et des jugements portés sur les grands écrivains qui l'ont illustré... J'espère que tous les poètes vont se lever. [43]

The question of *Ubu*, rather than that of the Symbolist Movement and the literary taste of an epoch, however, remained uppermost. Some of the admirers of *Ubu* went so far as to say that it did not matter who wrote the play, that it was and would remain a masterpiece no matter who the supposed author was. For example, André Thérive declared: "Bref, *Ubu*, ainsi découronné de son mystère, rendu à son auteur, n'en est pas moins indestructible et la parcelle du génie qu'il contient reste entière." [44] Lugné-Poe defended his friend Jarry but also maintained that authorship of the play was not really important:

---

[42] "Les Livres: *Les Sources d'Ubu Roi,* par Charles Chassé," *Les Marges,* 23, No. 91 (January 15, 1922), 63. We might mention here that Chassé does quote a very puzzling letter by Charles Morin published in *La Dépêche de Brest* in November, 1921, in which Morin denies being the author of *Ubu Roi* and admits to having no literary talent: "... n'étant nullement littéraire, comment aurais-je pu pondre cette œuvre où les 'princes de la critique' ont retrouvé le génie de Shakespeare et d'Aristophane?" See Chassé, *op. cit.,* p. 81. Chassé treats the letter as a joke but might there not be some truth in it?

[43] Quoted in Chassé, *op. cit.,* pp. 79-80.

[44] "Le Mystère d'*Ubu Roi,*" *L'Opinion,* 14ᵉ année, No. 50 (December 10, 1921), 651-652.

Farce de collégien, ou satire sociale, que nous importe! C'est le résultat qui inté-
resse.... Que M. Chassé nous affirme qu'*Ubu* n'est qu'une "quasi mystification,"
peu nous chaut. Il fut autre chose.

Il fut une œuvre réelle et le théâtre en tira une large part d'intelligence et
de foi.... Une expérience prochaine nous apprendra si cette "quasi-mystifica-
tion" répond aussi bien à notre état d'âme actuel qu'à celui de 1888. [45]

The "expérience prochaine" was the revival of *Ubu Roi* at the
Théâtre de l'Œuvre in February, directed by Lugné-Poe himself and
featuring René Fauchois and Jane Pierly as Père and Mère Ubu. Advance
publicity predicted that it would be "Le Triomphe d'Ubu" and cardboard
figures of Ubu, based on the drawings by Jarry, were distributed in the
streets.

The recent Fasquelle re-edition of the play was used as the working
text but several alterations, primarily deletions, were made by Lugné-
Poe for the production. [46] The first three acts remained almost intact
except for parts of a few speeches, but in Acts IV and V, several entire
scenes were deleted. They include the rout of Mère Ubu by Bougrelas
and his partisans (IV, ii); the episode of the bear (IV, vi and parts of
V); Ubu's dream (IV, vii); and all of V, iii.

Titles completely unrelated to the action of the play were given to
each of the five acts:

Act I. "Couronnement de Molière."
Act II. "Les Pêcheurs à la ligne."
Act III. "La Toilette de la Mariée."
Act IV. "La Fête de Cérès."
Act V. "L'Œil de Moscou." [47]

As recommended by Jarry for the original production of the play, changes
of locale were announced by printed *pancartes* or by mere suggestions of

---

[45] "La Semaine Théâtrale: A propos d'*Ubu Roi*," *L'Eclair* (January 10,
1922), 3.

[46] See Ruth B. York, "Ubu Revisited, Reprise of 1922," in *French Review*,
25 (1962), 408-411, for a complete list of revisions based on a copy of the play
labeled "Conduite-Mise-en-scène" and annotated in Lugné-Poe's handwriting.

[47] York, *op. cit.*, p. 408. In reference to the title for Act I, Professor York
commented: "The enormous tercentenary festival of Molière, including the crown-
ing of the bust, had been held in 1922."

scenery. For example, the stage direction for III, vi, reads: "Un palotin apporte une silhouette du palais." [48]

The mise-en-scène of the Œuvre production of *Ubu Roi* was generally applauded by the critics. G. S., the critic for *L'Illustration,* wrote in his review:

Cette farce énorme... est montée cette fois avec une originalité et un luxe assez impressionants. L'action se déroule devant des tableaux à personnages vivants, mais muets, qui n'ont pas de rapport avec elle, mais qui sont comme un rappel d'actualité symbolique: couronnement du buste de Molière, conférences diplomatiques, signatures de traités officiels, etc.... C'est bizarre, imprévu, ahurissant, pas ennuyeux grâce à la musique de Claude Terrasse. [49]

But the "belle reprise" of *Ubu Roi* was not at all the "Triomphe d'Ubu" that Lugné-Poe and the supporters of the play had hoped for; in fact it was a total failure.

Fernand Vandérem described the disastrous "répétition générale":

La répétition générale d'*Ubu Roi,* à l'Œuvre, a été un triomphe, — j'entends pour ses détracteurs.

Tous ceux qui, à l'occasion d'une réédition récente, s'étaient déchaînés dans des articles contre la pièce de Jarry, rayonnaient d'orgeuil devant une telle confirmation de leurs éreintements. Aux entr'actes, des groupes flatteurs se formaient autour d'eux et leur prodiguaient des félicitations qu'ils acceptaient sans fausse modestie. On percevait des "bravo, mon cher!," des "Eh bien! vous êtes content!," des "Cette fois, ça y est!," enfin toute la gamme des phrases classiques dont on encense l'auteur d'une pièce à succès. J'ai même entendu mieux, quelqu'un qui disait à l'un des vainqueurs: "Vous êtes l'homme de la soirée!"

Et c'était exact. Ils ont été les hommes de la soirée: un désastre, un échec comme de ma vie je n'en ai vu, une salle de glace, pas même en fin d'acte ces applaudissements qui partent tout seuls, fût-ce aux pires fours. [50]

Lugné-Poe later tried gallantly to take the blame for the failure of the play:

Appelé à Madrid par des représentations, je dus laisser à René Fauchois le soin d'achever les répétitions.... La pièce glissa en mon absence vers la farce d'atelier. La satire ne porta pas; erreur de mise-en-scène, de distribution dont je reste seul coupable. [51]

---

[48] *Ibid.,* p. 409.

[49] "Les Théâtres," *L'Illustration* (March 4, 1922), 211.

[50] "Les Lettres et la Vie," *Revue de France* (March 15, 1922), 403-404.

[51] *Parade: Dernière pirouette* (Paris: Sagittaire, 1946), p. 143.

But the detractors of *Ubu Roi* put all the blame on the play itself. André Beaunier, writing in *L'Echo de Paris*, was quite vehement:

Qu'est-il donc arrivé? Il y avait le roi Ubu: le roi Ubu est mort.... Aucun enthousiasme, l'ennui, le seul ennui devant le triste néant.... Quant à décider s'il faut jouer ainsi cet *Ubu Roi*, je me récuse et dirais plutôt qu'il ne faut pas le jouer du tout. [52]

Adolphe Brisson even went so far as to describe his boredom in verse:

Ce fut la chute morne
De l'ennuyeux parfait devant l'ennui sans borne. [53]

However, Brisson, unlike the other detractors of the play, did grant it a certain amount of historical importance:

Cette œuvre bruyante et paradoxale, qui aujourd'hui passerait à peu près inaper- çue, contribua à émanciper le théâtre; elle l'affranchit des pudeurs, des conve- nances, des retenues de langage, des timidités dont il s'était embarrassé au cours de trois siècles de goût et d'élégance; elle le ramena au ton des Parades du Pont-Neuf.... Alfred Jarry fut, à ce point de vue, un novateur. [54]

There were many others who did continue to admire and praise the play in spite of the obvious failure of its recent revival. Vandérem con- cluded his account of the disastrous "répétition générale" with a profes- sion of faith in the literary merits and lasting qualities of the play:

Mais ils ont bien fait de profiter de cette soirée, car, dès le lendemain, c'étaient celles d'*Ubu* qui recommençaient, sinon au théâtre, sinon devant les spectateurs, chez nous, aux rayons de notre bibliothèque, dans notre souvenir et dans nos entretiens. Car, qu'on écrive contre eux tout ce qu'on voudra, — scatalogique, puéril, grossier, absurde, — Ubu, la Mère Ubu, le capitaine Bordure, continueront de vivre de cette vie éternelle que confère la littérature aux types qu'elle a adop- tés comme siens, toujours présents dans notre esprit, dans nos impressions, dans nos propos, quand surgiront devant nous la laideur, la peur, la bassesse, tout ce que le vice offre de comique ou de vil. [55]

---

[52] Quoted in Chassé, *op. cit.*, p. 96.

[53] Adolphe Brisson, "Alfred Jarry: *Ubu Roi* (reprise)," *Le Théâtre*, 3ᵉ Série, 233-234.

[54] *Ibid.*, p. 235.

[55] Vandérem, *op. cit.*, p. 404.

Those who defended the play tended also to defend Jarry as author of the play. In a review of Jarry's adaptation of "The Rime of the Ancient Mariner," André Fontainas took advantage of the opportunity to pay homage to the memory of Alfred Jarry and to discuss *Ubu Roi*:

> Certes, *Ubu Roi* a pu, l'auteur et ses amis en faisant part volontiers, n'être qu'une farce d'écolier. Que nous importe? et que viennent faire là les prétendus auteurs primitifs levés soudain on ne sait d'où, pour en revendiquer la gloire? Si l'élève Jarry n'a pas imaginé, le premier, le type d'Ubu — c'est bien possible, — ni même la forme volontairement boursoufflé et grandiose de cette parodie, — c'est lui, avec l'effarante pénétration de son savoir linguistique, de sa sureté et son abondance verbale, qui a su, tout simplement métamorphoser une parodie, une farce d'écolier en une œuvre de portée universelle, cinglante et vengeresse. [56]

Thus not even the failure of the revival of *Ubu Roi* could help Charles Chassé accomplish his triple purpose of discrediting Jarry, the play, and, by a complicated process of association, the entire Symbolist Movement. Jarry continued to be considered the major, if not the sole, author of *Ubu Roi*; the play itself continued to be appreciated and to exert an increasing influence on the theater and the other arts; and the Symbolist Movement never even felt the blow of Chassé's determined but weak assault.

There were no further productions or re-editions of the Ubu plays for several years. In September, 1937, *Ubu enchaîné* finally received its first performance by the "Compagnie du Diable Ecarlate" at the Comédie des Champs-Elysées. The printed program included texts by André Breton, Paul Eluard, Sylvain Ithine, and others, and drawings by Picasso, Yves Tanguy, Roger Blin, and Miró. Fasquelle then republished the play in 1938 in an edition that included *Ubu sur la Butte,* and Jarry's articles "Les Paralipomènes d'Ubu," "Questions de théâtre," and "De l'inutilité du théâtre au théâtre."

Ubu Cocu was finally published in 1944 by the Editions des Trois Collines in Geneva from a manuscript that belonged to Paul Eluard. Its first performance came two years later in May, 1946, in a student production that received little attention from the public.

In the spring of 1945, *Ubu Roi* was revived at another of the avant-garde theaters, the Vieux-Colombier. Again, the production was less than

---

[56] "Les Poèmes," *Mercure de France,* 155 (April-May, 1922), 752.

a success. This time the critics expressed disappointment with both the production and the play itself. In 1947, *Ubu Roi* was re-edited in Paris by Marcel Sautier. The following year the *Œuvres complètes* of Jarry were published by the Editions du Livre in Monté-Carlo and Henri Kaeser in Lausanne. Unfortunately, there are many errors and omissions in this edition. Perhaps an even more important event in the career of Jarry and Ubu took place in 1948 and 1949, the founding of the Collège de 'Pataphysique whose members are dedicated to the propagation and elucidation of the works of Jarry in their *Cahiers* and *Dossiers*.

Ubu was also beginning to attract attention outside of France. In 1942, *VVV*, a surrealist magazine in New York edited by David Hare, André Breton, and Max Ernst, published a translation of parts of "Guignol." And in December, 1945, a translation of Acts I and II of *Ubu Cocu* by Cyril Connolly appeared in *Horizon*. Inspired by the season and the era, Connolly called Ubu, as I have already noted, "the Santa Claus of the Atomic Age." The first English translation of *Ubu Roi*, by Barbara Wright, was published in 1951 in London by the Gaberbochus Press and in New York by New Directions. The translation itself is quite pedestrian but the line drawings on every page by Francisca Themerson are excellent. This edition has had several reprintings and is still available. The year 1952 witnessed performances of *Ubu* in both London and New York. The London production, directed by William Jay, used the Wright translation. The masks and program were designed by Themerson. The New York production at the Cherry Lane Theater in August used an unpublished translation credited to Jane Warren and Arnold Deorce, supposed to be the pen names of Judith Malina and Julian Beck.

One of the most successful productions of *Ubu* was the one given in Paris by the Théâtre National Populaire directed by Jean Vilar. The T.N.P. presented an *Ubu* that combined *Ubu Roi, Ubu enchaîné*, and *Ubu sur la Butte*. There were two series of performances of this *Ubu*, the first series of thirty-two performances in March and April, 1958, and the second series of nine performances in November and December, 1960.

The proof that Ubu had finally reached the general public came in 1962 when the Librairie Générale Française published in a Livre de Poche edition *Tout Ubu* which included all the Ubu plays, the fragments of *Onésime* and *Ubu Cocu ou l'Archéoptéryx*, the *Almanachs du Père Ubu*, and all of Jarry's writings on the theater. This edition was very well documented by Maurice Saillet who used the work of J. H. Sainmont; both Saillet and Sainmont are members of the Collège de 'Pataphysique. This same edition was reprinted in hard cover by Fasquelle in 1968. This is undoubtedly the best edition of the Ubu plays to date.

Another English translation of the play, entitled *King Turd,* by Beverly Keith and G. Legman was published by Boar's Head Books in New York in 1953. Michael Benedikt and George Wellwarth have also translated the play into English. This translation, entitled simply *King Ubu,* is included in their edition of *Modern French Theater* published in New York by E. P. Dutton and Co. in 1964.

Growing interest in Jarry's work prompted the *Evergreen Review* to devote a complete issue to Jarry and his followers in the Collège de 'Pataphysique. The issue, entitled "'Pataphysics is the Only Science," appeared in May-June, 1960, and was edited by Roger Shattuck and Simon Watson Taylor. In 1965, Shattuck and Taylor edited a *Selected Works of Alfred Jarry* also published by Grove press. It included the first complete translation of *Ubu Cocu* as well as English versions of a selection of Jarry's other writings. Finally, in 1968, Grove Press published *The Ubu Plays* edited by Cyril Connolly and Simon Watson Taylor. It contains translations of all three of the Ubu plays and they are the best translations of these plays that we have.

Ubu Roi was again presented in London in the summer of 1966 at the Royal Court Theater in an adaptation by Ian Cuthbertson. The most notable aspect of this production was the fact that Mère Ubu was played by a man. This was a tradition that had evidently begun with some of the student productions of *Ubu Roi* and *Ubu Cocu* in Paris.

In the summer of 1968, *Ubu Roi* was given a fairly successful production in New York by a visiting repertory company from Yugoslavia. The play was performed in Serbo-Croatian with simultaneous translation into English. This technique, although a simple result of circumstance, must have indeed added both a new comic dimension and a new symbolic suggestiveness to the play.

The lasting qualities of *Ubu* and the growing recognition of Jarry as a key figure in modern French literature were well demonstrated during the Parisian theatrical season of 1970-1971. The month of October, 1970, witnessed both the opening of a revival of *Ubu Roi* and the opening of a new production, written, produced, and directed by Jean-Louis Barrault, entitled *Jarry sur la Butte*, [57] that was a tribute to Jarry and to his works. It included the presentation of excerpts from his play and novels as well as the dramatization of incidents from his life. The revival of *Ubu* was probably the most successful, although not necessarily the most authentic, production the play has yet received. It was performed with great gusto by a young, avant-garde company called "Le Phénoménal Théâtre" with J.-Pierre Lavabre in the title role. A great deal of the success of the production was due to the performance of Marie Pillet in the role of Mère Ubu although her interpretation of the role was quite different from the original conception of Jarry. No longer do we find a hideous hag but a young, energetic, and not entirely unattractive slut who is more interested in seducing Ubu's henchmen than in becoming Queen of Poland. The play is changed considerably, and undoubtedly Jarry would have objected to this injection of sexuality into the production as an opportunistic effort to appeal to the prurient tastes of the theater-going public. He would probably have been correct in this assessment of the motive for adding sexual interest to the play, but, on the other hand, it did seem to be effective. When the Théâtre de Plaisance closed for the summer, the production of *Ubu* moved to the Théâtre du Mouffetard where it continued to attract sizable audiences after an already record run of ten months.

Gallimard has finally begun the publication of a critical edition of Jarry's *Œuvres* in its "Bibliothèque de la Pléiade" series. The first volume, edited with notes and commentary by Michel Arrivé, was published in 1972. One might conclude that Jarry has now been recognized as a major figure in the history of French literature.

---

[57] The text of this production with notes indicating the manner of staging was published in 1970 by Gallimard.

II

PLOT STRUCTURE AND EPISODES

The fact that *Ubu Roi* began as a schoolboy satire and was performed often as a puppet play explains many of the plot features. The play does have a recognizable plot although it is exaggeratedly simple. The major action is the assassination of a king and the usurpation of his throne. The development of the action is characterized by an unusual and, we might add, unrealistic directness which has the earmarks of parody. The play begins with the decision by Ubu to assassinate King Venceslas and proceeds without interruption or hesitation through the deed and its consequences.

The idea to assassinate the king is introduced as early as the fourth line of the play. Père Ubu has characteristically threatened his wife: "Que ne vous assom-je, Mère Ubu!" (I, i). But Mère Ubu slyly replies: "Ce n'est pas moi, Père Ubu, c'est un autre qu'il faudrait assassiner" (I, i). Père Ubu hesitates only momentarily, out of cowardice and stubbornness rather than from any honorable motives, but by appealing to his greed, Mère Ubu easily convinces him to murder the king and usurp the throne. By the end of the first scene, she correctly predicts what is to come:

Vrout, merdre, il a été dur à la détente, mais vrout, merdre, je crois pourtant l'avoir ébranlé. Grâce à Dieu et à moi-même, peut-être dans huit jours serai-je reine de Pologne. (I, i)

By the end of Act I, the conspirators have been enlisted and the plan formulated. By the second scene of Act II, the plot has been carried out and Père Ubu is the new king of Poland.

The remaining action of the play is equally direct. In very few scenes, Ubu has massacred all the nobles and magistrates and has ravaged the countryside collecting double and triple taxes from the peasants. But he is finally defeated by the Russian army whose aid has been enlisted by one of the former conspirators and by the partisans of Bougrelas, sole surviving heir of the former king. The play ends as Ubu and his band flee on a ship toward France where the indomitable Ubu threatens to become "Maître des Finances à Paris" (V, iv).

One of the results of the directness or abruptness of action in the play is that it eliminates any feeling of mounting tension. We never have any doubt that, once Ubu has decided to assassinate the king, he will be able to do so. Moreover, no one action or episode is given any more emphasis than any other. The general significance of the plot tends to be devaluated. Rather than a feeling of suspense, the spectator experiences a kind of bemused curiosity as to what the great blustering fool, Ubu, will do next.

In spite of its seemingly episodic nature, the plot is carefully constructed. In accordance with the basic rules of dramatic structure, each event is prepared for in advance and each action leads logically to the next. For example, it is the king himself who gives the conspirators the opportunity to carry out their plan when he invites Ubu to be present at the military review (I, vi). It is also in this same scene that we become aware of young Bougrelas and of his dislike for Ubu. Because of his impertinence in this scene, the king later (II, i) forbids Bougrelas to be present at the review at which the king will be killed, a deed allowing Bougrelas to escape and leading ultimately to his victory over Ubu.

We are also prepared early in the play for Bordure's change of allegiance. In fact, from the very beginning when Ubu offers to make Bordure Duke of Lithuania in order to entice him to join the conspiracy, we suspect that Ubu has no intention of complying by the manner in which he stifles Mère Ubu's objections to his sudden generosity. Our suspicions are confirmed as soon as Ubu has become king. Immediately after the celebration of his coronation (III, i) Ubu admits that he has no further use for Bordure and does not intend to give him the duchy. Again it is Mère Ubu who predicts what is to come: "Tu as grand tort, Père Ubu, il va se tourner contre toi" (III, i). Furthermore, Mère Ubu is aware of the threat posed by the very existence of Bougrelas and attempts to warn her husband of this second danger, but this action is to no avail.

We are not surprised, then, to learn three scenes later that Bordure has in fact turned against Ubu because of Ubu's failure to carry out his original promise. Ubu has imprisoned Bordure in a supposedly impregnable fortification, but in the very next scene we find Bordure at the court of the Czar of Russia in the act of enlisting his aid to oust Ubu and restore Bougrelas to the throne. From this point on, Ubu's defeat is inevitable.

Perhaps it would be advisable, in view of the episodic nature of the plot, to give a detailed outline of the action.

Act. I. Preparations for the assassination.

    sc.   i. Mère Ubu plants the suggestion in Ubu's mind.

    sc.   ii, iii, iv. The conspirators' dinner. Ubu enlists the aid of Bordure and his men.

    sc.   v. A messenger tells Ubu that he is summoned by the king.

    sc.   vi. Venceslas rewards Ubu and invites him to a review the following day.

    sc.   vii. The conspirators formulate their plans.

Act II. The assassination and surrounding events.

    sc.   i. The queen expresses her fears for her husband's life. The king ignores them and forbids Bougrelas to attend the review of the troops. He departs with Ladislas and Boleslas. [1]

    sc.   ii. At the review. Ubu and his men kill the king and set off in pursuit of his sons who have fled.

    sc.   iii. The Palace. Bougrelas and the queen witness the death of Ladislas and Boleslas.

    sc.   iv. Ubu and his men break into the palace but Bougrelas and the queen manage to escape.

    sc.   v. A cavern in the mountains to which Bougrelas and the queen have retreated. The queen dies. The ghosts of the entire family appear and incite Bougrelas to revenge.

    sc.   vi. Bordure and Mère Ubu persuade Ubu to give a feast in celebration of his having become king.

    sc.   vii. The celebration.

---

[1] There is an inconsistency in time here. In I, vi, Venceslas invites Ubu to attend the review the *following* day. But in II, i, Venceslas speaks of the former scene as having taken place "*ce* matin" and yet departs immediately for the review.

Act. III.   Ubu the king, his actions, and the beginnings of a revolt against him.

sc.   i.   Mère Ubu warns Ubu about Bordure and Bougrelas. He ignores her.
sc.   ii. Ubu condemns the nobles and magistrates in order to steal their riches.
sc.   iii. A peasant's house. The peasants discuss the actions of Ubu. Ubu arrives.
sc.   iv. Ubu demands the payment of double and triple taxes. The peasants refuse. Ubu destroys their house.
sc.   v.   Ubu puts Bordure in prison.
sc.   vi. At the court of the Czar of Russia. Bordure persuades the Czar to help overthrow Ubu.
sc.   vii. Ubu speaks of affairs of state. He learns of the imminent attack on him by the Russian army.
sc.   viii. Ubu prepares for war. He leaves Mère Ubu in charge. She plans to steal the treasure.

Act IV.   War.

sc.   i.   Mère Ubu attempts to steal the treasure but is frightened away.
sc.   ii. Bougrelas rallies his supporters. They pursue Mère Ubu who flees.
sc.   iii. In the Ukraine. Ubu and his men prepare for battle with the Russians.
sc.   iv. The Battle. Defeat and flight of Ubu.
sc.   v.   A cavern to which Ubu has retreated with Pile and Cotice.
sc.   vi. Fight with a bear. Ubu sleeps. Pile and Cotice leave.
sc.   vii. Ubu dreams.

Act V.   Final defeat of Ubu.

sc.   i.   Ubu still sleeps. Mère Ubu enters and pretends to be an apparition.
sc.   ii. Bougrelas enters, a battle ensues, and "Les Ubs" flee.
sc.   iii. Flight of "Les Ubs." Ubu renounces the throne.
sc.   iv. "Les Ubs" flee by ship.

Parody is one of the major elements of the comedy of *Ubu Roi* and it is present on all levels of the play: in the basic plot, in the action of the individual episodes, in characterization and dialogue. At the present time, I will deal with parody only in so far as the plot and action are concerned.

On the most basic level, the major action of the play, the assassination of a king by an evil usurper and the usurper's downfall, is obviously the parody of a plot of high tragedy. In fact, the motto on the dedication page written in pseudo-archaic French suggests that some of the seeds of the plot of *Ubu Roi* might have come from the tragedies of Shakespeare: "Adonc le Père Ubu hoscha la poire, dont fut depuis nommé par les Anglois Shakespeare, et avez de lui sous ce nom maintes belles tragœdies par escript." The main action of the play parallels that of *Macbeth* and, indeed, Ubu, like Macbeth, is tempted to his crime by his ambitious wife. In Bougrelas we might find a mock-heroic counterpart of Hamlet, especially in the scene in which Bougrelas is enjoined to vengeance by the ghosts of his ancestors. As in *Julius Caesar,* the queen has a foreboding dream the night before the assassination and pleads with her husband not to attend the review; but Venceslas, like Caesar, refuses to heed her warning.

Parody is worked into the very structure of the play. The elements which would function as dramatic irony in the structure of the action in a tragedy become in *Ubu Roi* a parody of the same: Venceslas gives the conspirators the opportunity to carry out the assassination while at the same time preparing for the ultimate downfall of the usurper.

Parody is also a major element in the individual episodes. There are certain types of scenes or episodes that are traditional to a plot or action of high drama and suspense. If the plot concerns a conspiracy, we can almost expect one of the episodes to be a banquet or some similar gathering at which the conspirators are united to plan their evil deeds. We find just such a dinner in *Ubu Roi* with certain unique elements which completely remove it from the realm of serious drama. For example, in the scene which precedes the entrance of the other conspirators, there is comic action in and around Ubu's efforts to steal some food from the table. In order to divert Mère Ubu's attention from his actions, he plays the oldest of tricks on her; he tells her to go to the window to see if the others are arriving. While she is looking intently out of the window, he takes some food. But just at that moment, she turns around, catches him in the act, and begins to scream: "Ah! le veau! le veau! veau! Il a mangé le veau! au secours!" (I, ii). One can easily imagine that these lines are accompanied by equally exaggerated gestures. As we might expect, the other conspirators arrive right in the middle of this ridiculous scene of family strife.

The buffoonery continues throughout the dinner itself. Even the menu reflects the farcical tone of the episode:

Soupe polonaise, côtes de rastron, veau, poulet, pâté de chien, croupions de dinde, charlotte russe, bombe, salade, fruits, dessert, bouilli, topinambours, choux-fleurs à la merdre. (I, iii)

The manner in which the meal is consumed is reminiscent of a children's tea party, with quite unruly children, one might add. Rather than actually eat the food, they merely pretend to taste each dish, making appropriate comments as they do so, such as "Bougre, que c'est mauvais!" (I, iii) or "Il est très bon, j'ai fini" (I, iii). As usual, it is Père Ubu who interjects the most vulgar note of all. In the middle of the meal, he disappears from the room to return with "un balai innommable," throws it on the table, and invites all to "Goûtez un peu" (I, iii). After several have sampled it and supposedly fallen over dead, Ubu decides that it is time to conspire with Bordure and brusquely invites the others to leave: "A la porte tout le monde! Capitaine Bordure, j'ai à vous parler" (I, iii). When they all refuse because they have not finished their dinner, he begins to hurl *côtes de rastron* at them, accompanied by his favorite oath, and finally chases them out. The ludicrousness of the entire sequence completely removes any seriousness from the conspiracy itself, thus adding to the basic parody of the plot as well as presenting a broad farcical episode.

Other traditional scenes that are parodied in *Ubu Roi* include the military review, the battles and hand-to-hand combats, Ubu's dream, the fight with the bear, and the voyage by water with which the play ends. The comic effect is achieved in each one by the skillful use of stock comic devices, such as slapstick, vulgarity, threats, violence, and especially pantomime.

It has already been mentioned that pantomime was used in the dinner scene. The technique of merely suggesting an action or a scene is used throughout the play and is one of its most original aspects. In his letter to Lugné-Poe, Jarry made specific suggestions to this effect:

2° Une tête de cheval en carton qu'il [Ubu] se pendrait au cou, comme dans l'ancien théâtre anglais, pour les deux seules scènes équestres, tous détails qui étaient dans l'esprit de la pièce, puisque j'ai voulu faire un guignol....

... ...

4° Suppression des foules, lesquelles sont souvent mauvaises à la scène et gênent l'intelligence. Ainsi un seul soldat dans la scène de la revue, un seul dans la bousculade où Ubu dit: "Quel tas de gens, quelle fuite, etc...." [2]

---

[2] In *Tout Ubu*, pp. 123-124.

These same devices are used in the scene of Ubu's coronation (II, vii) in which Ubu distributes gold to his new subjects and then calls for a footrace of all the people and gives a chest of gold to the winner. The footrace in particular must be pantomimed for obvious technical reasons.

Pantomime and slapstick also play a major role in the two battle scenes and the numerous minor combats. In fact, no less than seven fights or battles take place in the course of the play. And they often terminate with the flight of one or two persons who are vigorously pursued by their adversaries, in other words, a classic comic chase.

The first such struggle takes place when Ubu and his partisans assassinate the king. The king conveniently dies at the first blow with a melodramatic "Oh! au secours! Sainte Vièrge, je suis mort" (II, ii). His two sons, Boleslas and Ladislas immediately take flight with Ubu, Bordure, and the others in hot pursuit. The next scene gives us an example of another age-old theatrical device. Rather than actually having the chase take place on stage, it is described and pantomimed for us by the queen and Bougrelas who witness it from the palace window. The noise offstage grows louder and louder until finally the door bursts open and Père Ubu, Bordure, and company rush in brandishing their swords. A mock-heroic duel ensues from which Bougrelas, a boy of fourteen, emerges the victor. He kills first one soldier; then as several advance, he kills them all with one blow using the "windmill" technique. With his final thrust before he and his mother escape by a secret stairway, he rips open the front of Ubu's costume, gallantly declaring as he does so: Ah! vive Dieu! Voilà ma vengeance!" (II, iv).

The scene of the battle between Ubu and the Russian army provides a fitting climax for this uproarious farce. It is the climax of the plot in the classic sense that it is the turning point of the action. Ubu's fortunes have risen steadily since the beginning of the play, but from this point on they will just as steadily decline until his final expulsion from Poland with which the play ends. The entire battle sequence also provides one of the high points in the comedy of the play.

The action is mainly determined by the comical traits which show the ruthlessness and cowardice of Ubu. Ubu cuts a truly ridiculous figure as warrior king throughout the action. As Mère Ubu said when he departed for war: "On dirait une citrouille armée" (III, viii). In the scene before the battle (IV, iii), Ubu comes on stage in a state of exhaustion dragging his horse behind him and complaining loudly. Nicholas Rensky approaches with the news that the Poles have revolted and chased Mère Ubu out of the capital. At the same time, they see the Russian army advancing across the plain below them. Since there is no possibility of escape (Ubu frankly admits that he would run without a fight if he could), Ubu makes an elaborate plan to defend the hill. He himself intends to take refuge in a windmill on the very top of the hill with his men all around him. However, a bullet arrives and breaks an arm of the windmill. The Russians have attacked. Other bullets begin to rain around them and Ubu, realizing that his position is not as secure as he has hoped, reluctantly decides to join the battle.

Naturally, we see only isolated incidents of the battle, in keeping with the basic principle of suggestion. In one incident, a Russian soldier fires a revolver at Ubu who begins immediately to wail and moan as if he is dying; then, when he realizes that he is not even hit, he turns on the Russian and fells him with one blow. This action is obviously in line with the broad farce which abounds in the play.

The high point of the scene comes in the encounter between Ubu and the Czar. Strangely enough, it is Ubu who initiates the fight by attacking the Czar but not out of any great upsurge of courage or heroism. The bottle of wine that Ubu always keeps in his pocket has been broken; so, on a casual suggestion from General Lascy, Ubu sets off to steal the Czar's bottle. As usual, Ubu's motives are greed, gluttony, cowardice, and fear. He attacks the Czar with great bravado, but as soon as the Czar begins to defend himself, Ubu turns tail and runs with the Czar pursuing him. Here, then, is another example of a chase. We must remember, too, that it is on horseback, and consequently the effect of the pantomime is enhanced. Ubu is saved only by a ditch which he jumps with his eyes closed but into which the Czar falls. The Russian soldiers must take time out from the battle to rescue their leader, and this action gives Ubu the opportunity to escape while Lascy is not looking. It is at this point that we have the pantomime of the army in flight when Ubu says: "Quel tas de gens, quelle fuite," etc.

I have already discussed the basic structural unity of the play. However, two of the most comic scenes, besides the scene of the battle described above, do not have an integral function in the plot of the play in the sense that they do not actually advance the action. These are the scene with the bear and the scene in which Mère Ubu pretends to be an apparition. But neither scene is entirely unrelated to the major action. The scene with the bear is another episode in the complete rout of Ubu and his partisans. And in the apparition scene, Mère Ubu and Père Ubu are reunited before their final defeat by Bougrelas and their flight from Poland. In both scenes, the comedy of situation, of action, of character, and of language are welded together in a harmonious unit. And both scenes employ classic elements of comedy, parody, pantomime, slapstick, and the like to achieve their effect.

In the first scene, a bear enters the cave in which Ubu and his two Palotins, Pile and Cotice, have taken refuge after their disastrous encounter with the Russians. The bear attacks Cotice, Pile attacks the bear, but Ubu climbs on top of a rock and begins to say the Pater Noster while the fierce struggle goes on below him. There is a great deal of slapstick in the action as the two Palotins struggle with an obviously make-believe bear. The function of the scene is also to bring out character traits which are the predominant element of the play. Ubu is perched timorously on a rock babbling Latin prayers, not because he is religious but because it is an excuse not to join the fight. Finally Cotice manages to kill the bear with his pistol. As soon as Ubu sees that the bear is dead, he cuts off his prayer and climbs down from the rock. His courage, or rather his braggadocio, returns immediately, and he declares that it is really he who has saved the day.

Shortly afterwards, night falls, Ubu goes to sleep, and the Palotins, disgusted with Ubu's behavior, seize the opportunity to steal away. Act IV ends as Ubu dreams and talks in his sleep. As Act V opens, Mère Ubu, who has been expelled from Warsaw by Bougrelas and his partisans, enters the cave where Ubu is sleeping. Not seeing him, she gives a lengthy description of her recent adventures and misadventures. Ubu begins to awaken and starts talking again. Mère Ubu, realizing who it is, decides to take advantage of the darkness to pretend to be an apparition in order to make Ubu forgive her for her thievery.

The scene is obviously a parody of classic scenes of apparitions. For example, such a scene is found in Shakespeare's *Julius Caesar* when the ghost of Caesar appears to Brutus the night before battle. Here, however, the situation is quite comic. The idea of Mère Ubu pretending to be the Archangel Gabriel is indeed ridiculous and her motives for doing so add to the irony. Naturally, Ubu, who is no respecter of persons whether they be human or divine, does not react at all in the manner in which she has hoped. The dialogue that ensues is a true "ballet de paroles." Ubu counters each statement that Mère Ubu makes in her own defense with the grossest of insults. Here is a brief but typical example:

Mère Ubu. Monsieur Ubu, votre femme est adorable et délicieuse, elle n'a pas un seul défaut.
Père Ubu. Vous vous trompez, il n'y a pas un seul défaut qu'elle ne possède.
(V, i)

Unwittingly, Mère Ubu ends by telling Ubu exactly what he wants to know: that she has been stealing from him. Just as she does, the sun rises and he discovers her. The scene ends as Ubu threatens her with the traditional "dernier supplice" which includes "torsion du nez, arrachement des cheveux, pénétration du petit bout de bois dans les oneilles," etc. (V, i).

Perhaps the frequency of fights and battles in the play can be traced to the fact that the play was originally written and performed by a group of young schoolboys. And boys enjoy nothing so much as participating in or witnessing a fight whether it be real or make-believe. The manner of staging these fights also remains close to the traditional techniques of the marionette theater. This, too, is an important aspect of the origins of the play. Other evidences of its *guignolesque* origins can be found in several of the stage directions which call for actions that could not possibly be performed by live actors. For example, in the assassination scene, we read: "Tous frappent le roi, un palotin explose" (II, ii). And in the battle scene, we find several examples of one character tearing another in half: "Il le déchire" (IV, iv). Jarry did not lose sight of the *guignolesque* elements of the play when he apparently took it with him to Paris and began to revise it. And it did receive both private and public performances by marionettes. What was originally a natural result of circumstances gradually became the foundation for Jarry's theories of dramatic technique. [3] In turn, Jarry's theories and the techniques employed in *Ubu Roi* planted the seeds for a complete renovation of the modern theater.

Underneath the riotous buffoonery of the action, a sardonic vision of the world comes through. The parody is not entirely superficial; at moments it approaches satire. It is not by chance that Ubu kills a king

---

[3] See below, p. 106 ff.

and upsets a kingdom. The enormity of his crime does not affect us as it would in a tragedy like *Macbeth,* but the mockery does extend to the institutions which Ubu destroys with such apparent ease. And even though the forces of "law and order" are restored in Poland at the end of the play, still Ubu, the indomitable and unscrupulous puppet villain of mankind, escapes unharmed and unchastened and threatens to become "Maître des Finances à Paris." We have no doubt that he will succeed.

The structure and unity of the plot of *Ubu Roi* and the significance of the action it illustrates account in large part for the uncontested superiority of this play over either *Ubu Cocu* or *Ubu enchaîné.* In *Ubu Cocu* in particular, there is little connection between the different threads of the plot, probably because the play was compiled from several different plays that were current in the Ubu cycles at the Lycée de Rennes. Furthermore, none of the different elements of the plot of *Ubu Cocu* is of any great significance or interest — neither the cuckolding of Ubu, nor the impaling of Achras, nor the hunt for mummies in Egypt.

Neither can we say, however, that the plot and action of *Ubu Roi* are of primary significance. In fact plot is probably the least important aspect of the play. Its main function is to serve as a vehicle to display and reveal the character of Ubu. This is where the real satire lies. Even critics of the play recognized the fact that Jarry had created a new and lasting comic type in the figure of Ubu. An analysis of this type will be the substance of the following chapter.

III

UBU, THE COMIC TYPE

Jarry himself makes quite clear that the character of Ubu is the center and the very raison d'être of the play in an article entitled "Questions de théâtre" which appeared in *La Revue Blanche* on January 1, 1897, a few days after the original production of the play. He states:

Je pense qu'il n'y a aucune espèce de raison d'écrire une œuvre sous forme dramatique, à moins que l'on ait eu la vision d'un personnage qu'il soit plus commode de lâcher sur une scène que d'analyser dans un livre. [1]

It has been noted that the character of Ubu was based on a living model. Nevertheless the figure of Ubu is far from being a simple satire of an ineffectual and unfortunate professor of physics in a provincial French lycée. Ubu has retained only a vague physical resemblance to Monsieur Hébert and shares with him a few basic characteristics such as his "gourmandise" and his "dignité grotesque." In several of his writings on the theater, Jarry discussed the relationship between Monsieur Hébert and Ubu. In his Preliminary Address, Jarry described Ubu as

la déformation par un potache d'un de ses professeurs qui représentait pour lui tout le grotesque qui fût au monde. [2]

And in the "Paralipomènes d'Ubu" which appeared shortly before the first performance, he further emphasized and clarified the synthetic aspect of the figure of Ubu:

---

[1] In *Tout Ubu,* p. 139.
[2] *Ibid.,* p. 19.

Cette pièce ayant été écrite par un enfant, il convient de signaler, si quelques-uns y prêtent attention, le principe de synthèse que trouve l'enfant créateur en ses professeurs. [3]

The fact that Jarry and his collaborators borrowed freely from other literary works in the creation of their *cycle épique* also contributed to the character of Ubu. In Ubu we can find echoes of Falstaff, Panurge, le Roi Anarch, and many other comic types. Whether or not Ubu was specifically modeled on these characters is not as important, however, as the fact of their sharing traditional comic characteristics. Ubu also shares basic traits with traditional folk comic figures and, in particular, with the comic types associated with the marionette theater. He belongs to the same family as Pulcinella, Polichinelle, and Punch. Paul Souday commented:

Ubu existe précisément de la même façon que Polichinelle, Karaguez, Croque-mitaine, la mère Michel ou le père Lustucru. Sous ce nom vaseux et cette sil-houette de citrouille ignoble, on peut mettre tout ce qu'on veut, dans l'ordre de la muflerie truculente et de l'horreur burlesque. Ubu est éminemment un person-nage de guignol, et peut-être, dans cent ou deux cents ans, jouera-t-il les pre-miers rôles dans les petits théâtres des marionnettes. [4]

In fact, Ubu possesses characteristics of a type that can be traced as far back as ancient Greek comedy. This is the *alazon* or imposter who "[represents] the principle of overstatement, struts about in false security, venting his heavy wit and braggadocio on the *eiron*." [5] This same type reappears in Latin comedy as the *miles gloriosus,* the cowardly soldier who brags loudly and at great length about his non-existent courage, and in the *Commedia dell'arte* as Scaramaccio or Scaramouche. I have already described in detail two episodes, the battle between Ubu and the Russians and the scene with the bear, in which Ubu's cowardice and braggadocio are prominent.

Another characteristic that links Ubu to such comic types as Falstaff and Gargantua is his gluttony, aptly symbolized by his most salient physical characteristic, his belly or *gidouille*. Man has always seemed to think that the animal aspects of his nature are inferior to his mind or

---

[3] *Ibid.,* p. 151.
[4] Quoted in Rachilde, *Alfred Jarry,* p. 108.
[5] David Worcester, *The Art of Satire* (Cambridge, Mass.: Harvard University Press, 1940), p. 92.

spirit. A recurrent theme in theories of comedy since Aristotle is that the purpose of comedy is to ridicule these animal or bestial aspects of human nature. In accordance with this theory, Ubu is the very embodiment of the basest human instincts, or as Catulle Mendès said, "la bassesse de l'instinct érigée en tyrannie." [6] One of Ubu's favorite expressions, *cornegidouille,* signifies, according to Jarry, "par la puissance des appétits inférieurs." [7] Hunger being the most basic animal instinct, it is appropriate that gluttony or greed is Ubu's most important vice.

It is not without significance that Mère Ubu mentions food in attempting to persuade Ubu to murder the king of Poland and usurp the throne: "Tu pourrais ... manger fort souvent de l'andouille ... " (I, i). Nor is it surprising that Ubu unites the conspirators at a dinner and celebrates his coronation as king by overeating. His first comment on being king is typical: "De par ma chandelle verte, me voici roi de ce pays, je me suis déjà flanqué une indigestion et on va m'apporter ma grande capeline" (III, i). Ubu even takes time out for lunch while the Russian army is advancing to attack him; and he himself attacks the Czar of Russia for the sole purpose of stealing his wine when his own bottle has been broken. Eating and drinking to excess, when not actually demonstrated, are mentioned throughout the play.

But gluttony is only one aspect of Ubu's greed; he is avid to acquire riches of any kind. His decision to murder the king and usurp the throne is, as Mère Ubu foresaw, entirely motivated by greed and not at all by political ambition. His method of ruling the country is also designed solely for the purpose of increasing his own personal fortune. His first major decision is to kill all the nobles in order to seize their wealth. He then proceeds to massacre the magistrates and financiers who understandably oppose his program of revising the government. When Mère Ubu objects that he is killing everyone, he confidently replies: "Ne crains rien, ma douce enfant, j'irai moi-même, de village en village, recueillir les impôts" (III, ii). And in fact, he does set out with his Palotins to collect the double and triple taxes that he has levied on all his subjects. His entire program of government is summarized in a statement he makes to a peasant from whom he is attempting to collect taxes for the second time:

---

[6] Quoted in Jarry, *Tout Ubu,* p. 140.
[7] In *Tout Ubu,* p. 23.

... j'ai changé le gouvernement et j'ai fait mettre dans le journal qu'on paierait deux fois tous les impôts et trois fois ceux qui pourront être désignés ultérieurement. Avec ce système, j'aurai vite fait fortune, alors je tuerai tout le monde et je m'en irai. (III, iv)

Ironically, this act turns the peasants against him and contributes to his fall.

Ubu's greed is matched by his miserliness. Whenever he is forced to give anything away, he does so only under great protest. When Mère Ubu announces the menu for the conspirators' dinner, he objects loudly, like another Harpagon, undaunted even by the presence of his guests: "Eh! me crois-tu empereur d'Orient pour faire de telles dépenses?" (I, ii). His attitude does not change after he has become king. He agrees to give the traditional feast to celebrate his accession to the throne only after Mère Ubu and Bordure have convinced him that the people will not pay their taxes otherwise. He even refuses to spend any money on the war to defend himself against the Russian army which is trying to overthrow him:

Je ne veux pas donner d'argent. En voilà d'une autre! J'étais payé pour faire la guerre et maintenant il faut la faire à mes dépens. Non, de par ma chandelle verte, faisons la guerre, puisque vous en êtes enragés, mais ne déboursons pas un sou. (III, vii)

Ubu's miserliness is coupled with a total lack of gratitude to those who have helped him. Immediately after Bordure has agreed to join the conspiracy, a messenger arrives to tell Ubu that he is summoned by the king. Naturally, Ubu's first thought is that the king suspects their plot and he reacts like a true coward: "Oh! merdre, jarnicotonbleu, de par ma chandelle verte, je suis découvert, je vais être décapité! hélas! hélas!" (I, v). But then he has an idea that he thinks will save him and boldly announces it to them: "Je dirai que c'est la Mère Ubu et Bordure" (I, v). He does not even try to hide his own treachery. In the following scene, he enters the palace announcing: "Oh! Vous savez, ce n'est pas moi, c'est la Mère Ubu et Bordure" (I, vi). But it soon becomes obvious that the king suspects nothing and has, in fact, invited Ubu there to reward him for his services by making him Count of Sandomir. Not even this honor can deter Ubu from his plan; after thanking the king, Ubu adds in an aside: "Oui, mais, roi Venceslas, tu n'en seras pas moins massacré" (I, vi).

After the assassination of the king and coronation of Ubu, Mère Ubu mentions the debt of gratitude they owe Bordure (Ubu has promised to give Bordure the duchy of Lithuania for his part in the conspiracy), but Ubu bluntly replies: "Maintenant que je n'ai plus besoin de lui, il peut bien se brosser le ventre, il n'aura point son duché" (III, i).

Ubu's other vices are accompanied by an almost gratuitous ferocity. It has already been noted that he kills all the nobles in order to seize their possessions. Nor does he hesitate to put the government officials to death when they oppose him. He also takes great joy, an almost childish glee, in torturing or threatening to torture Mère Ubu. The play opens with a typical exchange between the two of them:

Père Ubu. Merdre!
Mère Ubu. Oh! voilà du joli, Père Ubu, vous estes [sic] un fort grand voyou.
Père Ubu. Que ne vous assom-je, Mère Ubu!

(I, i)

In fact, he threatens her with total or partial annihilation no less than eight times in the course of the play. The last threat, which occurs in the apparition scene, contains an enumeration of the unique tortures that comprise what Ubu calls "le dernier supplice":

Torsion du nez, arrachement des cheveux, pénétration du petit bout de bois dans les oneilles [sic], extraction de la cervelle par les talons, lacération du postérieur, suppression partielle ou même totale de la moelle épinière . . . , sans oublier l'ouverture de la vessie natatoire et finalement la grande décollation renouvelée de saint Jean-Baptiste, le tout tiré des très saintes Ecritures, tant de l'Ancien que du Nouveau Testament, mis en ordre, corrigé et perfectionné par l'ici présent Maître des Finances! (V, i)

This "dernier supplice" was a traditional part of the *cycle ubique* current at the Lycée de Rennes and recurs in all of the Ubu plays. Equally traditional was the "Chanson du Décervelage," also included in the Ubu plays,[8] which describes in detail the weekly public ritual of "disembraining," another of Ubu's favorite tortures. Ubu's ferocity and the perverse pleasure he seems to derive from it can be attributed in part, then, to the origins of the play. Students who are attempting to

---

[8] The Revue Blanche edition of *Ubu Roi* in 1900 indicates that this song was to be sung at the end of the play. It occurs in Act III, sc. iii, of *Ubu Cocu* and in Act I of *L'Archéoptéryx*.

satirize a hated professor would naturally portray him as sadistic and vicious. And they would also take vicarious pleasure in imagining and acting out such viciousness. Brutality in the form of slapstick is also one of the oldest forms of comedy and is particularly present in the puppet theater. Ubu is, after all, an overgrown puppet, "ce gros pantin" as Mère Ubu calls him (III, viii).

Ubu's ferocity is just another aspect of his bestiality which is further enhanced by his unleashed obscenity in both word and action. The first word of the play which caused such an uproar on opening night, "merdre," is his characteristic response to anything that does not please him and is usually accompanied by threats or violence or both. I have already described the scene in which Ubu brings "le balai innommable" to the dinner table. Other scatological references are found throughout the play. For example, in the scene after the battle with the Russians, Pile asks Ubu: "Hon! Monsieur Ubu, êtes-vous remis de votre terreur et de votre fuite?" (IV, v), and Ubu answers: "Oui! Je n'ai plus peur, mais j'ai encore la fuite" (IV, v). Similarly, in the scene of the final battle with Bougrelas, when Pile says: "Courage, sire Ubu!" (V, ii), Ubu replies: "Ah! j'en fais dans ma culotte" (V, ii). The enjoyment of obscenity, like the enjoyment of brutality, is obviously a part of the adolescent mentality that first created Ubu. It is also a very basic element of comedy. This is another aspect of Ubu's character that relates him to other comic types such as Falstaff, Gargantua, and Polichinelle.

One of the few basic vices that Ubu does not possess is lust. In fact, the play is virtually devoid of any sexuality. The only reference to sex or love, and it is oblique, comes in the first scene of Act V. In her long monologue, Mère Ubu tells us that there was a romantic attachment between herself and the Palotin Giron whom Ubu had left to protect her when he went off to war:

Je perds mon cavalier le Palotin Giron qui était si amoureux de mes attraits qu'il se pâmait d'aise en me voyant, et même, m'a-t-on assuré, en ne me voyant pas, ce qui est le comble de la tendresse. (V, i)

Later in the scene when she is pretending to be an apparition, Mère Ubu attempts to deny this relationship to her husband: "Votre femme ne vous fait pas d'infidélités!" (V, i). Ubu's answer reveals his utter contempt for his wife and his complete disinterest in her fidelity or lack of it: "Je

voudrais bien voir qui pourrait être amoureux d'elle. C'est une harpie!"
(V, i). Even in *Ubu Cocu,* the title of which would lead us to expect a
great deal more eroticism, the "cocufication" of Ubu has only a secondary
role in the action of the play and, in fact, never takes place. The rumor
that Ubu will be betrayed by his wife serves primarily as an excuse for
him to practice "le dernier supplice" on her supposed lover.

Jarry himself noted with some irony and perhaps a little bitterness
that the lack of sexual interest on the one hand and the unrestrained
scatology on the other probably contributed to the public's negative reaction to the play. In "Questions de théâtre," he wrote:

Il aurait été aisé de mettre Ubu au goût du public parisien avec les légères mo-
difications suivantes: le mot initial aurait été Zut (ou Zutre), le balai qu'on ne
peut pas dire un coucher de petite femme, les uniformes de l'armée, du premier
Empire: Ubu aurait donné l'accolade au tsar et l'on aurait cocufié diverses per-
sonnes: mais ç'aurait été plus sale. [9]

It is perhaps surprising to note that Ubu is also completely without
guile. He never attempts to hide the base motives that underlie all his
actions, nor does he know how to court the favor of others in order
better to achieve his ends. We have already seen the manner in which
he treats Bordure and his men when he is trying to persuade them to
join the conspiracy. Nor does he try to hide from them the fact that he
will betray them at a moment's notice if he thinks he is in danger:
"Si je savais, je filerais vous dénoncer pour me tirer de cette sale affaire,
et je pense qu'il me donnerait aussi de la monnaie" (I, viii).

He is scarcely more polite with the king himself. For example,
when he is about to leave after his interview with the king, Ubu announces: "Et maintenant, je vais foutre le camp" (I, vi). As he is turning
to go, he falls and immediately begins to shout: "Oh! aïe! au secours!
De par ma chandelle verte, je me suis rompu l'intestin et crevé la bouzine! (I, vi). His vulgarity of language shows a complete lack of respect
for the king. One would have to be inordinately stupid or inordinately
naïve to be taken in by such a great fool as Ubu. Perhaps this is why
we feel little indignation at his killing of the king.

Once Ubu has become king, he does not attempt to win the support
of his subjects by showing any concern for their welfare. He frankly

---

[9] In *Tout Ubu,* p. 140.

admits to the people that he did not want to give the traditional feast to celebrate his coronation:

Tenez, voilà pour vous. Ça ne m'amusait guère de vous donner de l'argent, mais vous savez, c'est la Mère Ubu qui a voulu. Au moins, promettez-moi de bien payer les impôts. (II, vii)

He also makes no effort to disguise his base intentions to the men who run the government. He openly admits that his sole reason for killing the nobles and changing the government is to increase his own riches. And rather than attempting to appease the magistrates and financiers, he merely kills them when they oppose his plan.

Ubu's total lack of respect for persons or things includes even supernatural beings. In the scene in which Mère Ubu pretends to be the Archangel Gabriel, Ubu does show fear of her, but he is completely devoid of any awe. His responses to her statements and questions are quite impertinent, a fact which, of course, only adds to the comedy of the scene.

It is Ubu's guilelessness coupled with his overwhelming avarice that leads ultimately to his downfall. His refusal to give Bordure the duchy he has promised makes Bordure change his allegiance. And when Mère Ubu suggests that he would be wise to court the favor and support of Bougrelas "par des bienfaits" (III, i), Ubu replies: "Encore de l'argent à donner? Ah! non, du coup! vous m'avez fait gâcher bien vingt-deux millions" (III, i). We have already seen that his concern for the opinion of the people is equally lacking. Had he made the effort to play politics just a little, he probably would not have been defeated quite so easily.

But, on the other hand, one may also say that this same guilelessness is his only saving grace. His motives are of the very lowest kind but, at least, he does not try to camouflage them as virtues. He is no Tartuffe. [10] It is one of the least objectionable aspects of his character and at the same time one of the most frightening.

One of the peculiar aspects of the nature of comedy is that the comic protagonist, while being the very embodiment of vice, frequently remains sympathetic. Falstaff, for all his obesity, slovenliness, obscenity, and cow-

---

[10] For a comparison of Ubu and Tartuffe, see Johnnie Lou Mathis, "Tartuffe and Ubu" (unpublished Master's thesis, University of Tennessee, 1966).

ardice, is so lovable that he is in danger of stealing the play from its true protagonist, young Prince Hal. The element of Falstaff's character that makes him so lovable — and this is true of most comic characters — is his indomitable love of life. In describing the traditional folk and literary type of the buffoon, Suzanne K. Langer points out:

It is true that the comical figures are often buffoons, simpletons, clowns; but such characters are almost always sympathetic, and although they are knocked around and abused, they are indestructible, and eternally self-confident and good-humored. [11]

Miss Langer goes on to say that a buffoon

is genuinely amoral — now triumphant, now worsted and rueful, but in his ruefulness and dismay he is funny, because his energy is really unimpaired and each failure prepares the situation for a new fantastic move. [12]

I believe I have already shown that Ubu possesses many characteristics of the buffoon; he is also essentially amoral. His drives are the basic instincts common to animals and man — hunger, self-preservation, and aggression — but blown-up and intensified to the point that they become what we normally call vices: gluttony, greed, cowardice, egotism, ferocity.

But Ubu lacks the one ingredient that would make him seem truly villainous and that is a real sense of right and wrong. Such a moral sense comes only from a recognition that social and ethical values supersede the biological facts of man's existence on earth. Ubu, although he does have at least a superficial awareness of the concepts of law and conscience, completely rejects them in an almost childlike manner if they come in conflict with his desires. When Mère Ubu attempts to convince her husband to try to win the support of Bougrelas "car il a pour lui le bon droit" (III, i), Ubu, who is afraid that he may have to share his wealth and glory, replies: "Ah! saleté! le mauvais droit ne vaut-il pas le bon?" (III, i). He wastes no time in dismissing any feeling of remorse.

A scene in *Ubu Cocu* also illustrates the question of conscience. Ubu consults his Conscience on an important matter, whether or not he should kill the man in whose house he has forcibly taken up residence. It is significant that Ubu's Conscience is portrayed as being a completely

---

[11] *Feeling and Form* (New York: Charles Scribner's Sons, 1953), p. 342.
[12] *Ibid.*

separate entity from his master; he is described as "un grand bonhomme en chemise" (I, iv) and is carried about in a suitcase. Here is the substance of their conversation:

Père Ubu. Nous allons prendre conseil de notre Conscience. Elle est là, dans cette valise, toute couverte de toiles d'araignée. On voit bien qu'elle ne nous sert pas souvent. (Il ouvre la valise. Sort la Conscience . . .)

… …

Répondez . . . à cette question: ferai-je bien de tuer Monsieur Achras, qui a osé venir m'insulter dans ma propre maison?

La Conscience. Monsieur, et ainsi de suite, il est indigne d'un homme civilisé de rendre le mal pour le bien. Monsieur Achras vous a hébergé, . . . Monsieur Achras, et ainsi de suite, est un fort brave homme, bien inoffensif, ce serait une lacheté, et ainsi de suite, de tuer un pauvre vieux incapable de se défendre.

… …

Père Ubu. Merci, Monsieur, nous n'avons plus besoin de vous. Nous tuerons Monsieur Achras, puisqu'il n'y a pas de danger, et nous vous consulterons plus souvent, car vous savez donner de meilleurs conseils que nous ne l'aurions cru. Dans la valise! (I, iv).

One cannot help admiring Ubu's facility at turning things to his own advantage.

Later in the same play, Ubu performs the symbolic act of "flushing" his conscience. He is without any sense of guilt and has no concern for the most basic social and ethical values. He is hardly even aware of their existence. To murder a king and usurp the throne literally mean no more to him than the opportunity to eat "andouille" every day. Ubu is basically an overgrown child, although a malicious one, and as such evokes in all of us the mirage of a return to a state of primeval innocence. The satire of *Ubu Roi* is double-edged.

Like the buffoon, Ubu is also indomitable, even though he does suffer defeat at the hands of the Russians and is finally forced to abandon the throne and flee the country. But his spirit is not conquered; he retains his joviality and his love of verbiage even during the flight from Poland. He also retains the same desires and determination he has had since the beginning of the play. He announces with great confidence: "Et moi je me ferai nommer Maître des Finances à Paris" (V, iv). He has learned nothing either from his success or his failure.

Another essential characteristic of the comic type is that it does not go through any character development. Again as Miss Langer points out:

"Because the comic rhythm is that of vital continuity, the protagonists do not change in the course of the play, as they normally do in tragedy." [13] The comic type represents or symbolizes basic and eternal human characteristics rather than particular individual characteristics which are more susceptible to change. A miser who ceases to be a miser is no longer a comic figure; Ubu reformed is no Ubu at all.

On the other hand, Jean Morienval has noted in his study on famous types in French literature that a true type cannot be too general or he lacks interest:

Le type littéraire doit être à la fois assez général et assez particulier. Si on ne lui donne que des traits qui s'appliquent à tous les personnages auxquels il doit servir de patron, le type ne vit pas; si ce qui domine chez lui est trop personnel, trop incident, il reste un personnage et ne peut être typifié. [14]

M. Morienval himself goes on to point out that Ubu fits the definition of a type very well. According to M. Morienval, one of the first requirements for creating a comic type is to christen him with a fitting name, one that reflects his character. The name Ubu, as many critics have remarked, was a particularly felicitous invention. And the character of Ubu, while embodying the most basic and general human vices — greed, egotism, ferocity, and cowardice — is unique in the very exaggeration of these vices and in his total incomprehension that they are vices. It is difficult to imagine even the most hardened criminal saying with the candor and innocence that Ubu does: "J'aurai vite fait fortune, alors je tuerai tout le monde et je m'en irai" (III, iv).

We know from his letter to Lugné-Poe and from the Preliminary Address that Jarry intended that the mask which is reminiscent of the *guignol* face be worn by the actor who played the role of Ubu: "Il a plu à quelques acteurs... de jouer enfermés dans un masque, afin d'être bien exactement l'homme intérieur et l'âme des grandes marionnettes que vous allez voir." [15] He thus gave added function and significance to an element which is only technically attached to the genre of pantomime. Jarry further defined his theory of dramatic characterization in an article on the characters of Henri de Régnier entitled "Du mimétisme inverse chez les personnages de Henri de Régnier":

---

[13] *Ibid.*, p. 335.
[14] *De Pathelin à Ubu*, p. 16.
[15] In *Tout Ubu*, p. 19.

Que chaque héros traîne après soi son décor, que nous ne voyons pas le Prince de Praizig sans sa redingote militaire, Madame de Vitry sans ses joues pelées ... ; cela prouve, sans plus, que l'auteur a retourné ses créatures et mis leur âme en dehors: l'âme est un tic. [16]

Johnnie L. Mathis correctly observes that Jarry

used the mask as a means of penetrating the visible reality in order to arrive at the "naked soul." ... The mask, as Jarry conceived it, would take from its wearer all indication of the temporal and human and would reflect what Jarry believed to be the innermost being, or soul, of all men; Jarry saw the soul as monstrous and grotesque. [17]

In the program distributed to the spectators at the Théâtre de l'Œuvre, Jarry had written: "Monsieur Ubu est un être ignoble, ce pourquoi il nous ressemble (par en bas) à tous." [18] And in "Les Paralipomènes d'Ubu," Jarry had said: "C'est un homme, d'où couardise, saleté, laideur, etc." [19]

Albert Cook has noted another difference between tragedy and comedy, and that is the relationship between the audience and the characters on stage. He states that in tragedy the relationship is basically third-personal, i.e., the characters on stage "are as objective to the spectators as if they were in a book." [20] But in comedy, on the other hand, the relationship is second-personal, i.e., the characters on stage address themselves directly to the audience. Admitting that this distinction is too absolute to correspond to all plays that might fit into the categories of tragedy or comedy, we may note that it happens to be applicable in some concrete instances to *Ubu Roi*. For example, Mère Ubu's soliloquy in the first scene of Act V is not a true soliloquy "addressed by the individual protagonist to his own soul" [21] as it would be in tragedy; she is instead talking directly to the members of the audience in order to bring them up-to-date on what has happened to her since they last saw her. Similarly, Ubu's speech after the Czar has fallen in a ditch during the battle, a

---

[16] In Alfred Jarry, *Œuvres complètes* (Monté-Carlo: Editions du Livre and Lausanne: Henri Kaeser, n. d. [1948]), VII, 137.

[17] "Tartuffe and Ubu," p. 24.

[18] In *Tout Ubu*, p. 21.

[19] *Ibid.*, p. 151.

[20] *The Dark Voyage and the Golden Mean* (Cambridge, Mass: Harvard University Press, 1949), p. 44.

[21] *Ibid.*, p. 45.

speech which ends with "Tout ceci est fort beau, mais personne ne m'écoute" (IV, iv), is also directed at the audience.

Irony in comedy becomes then "a second-personal joke between some of the characters and the audience; the butt of the joke can be either the abnormal character type or a member of the audience, . . ." [22] or both, as is the case in *Ubu Roi*. By the honest admission of his own vices, by his very enjoyment of them, Ubu is forcing us into complicity with him. Our protests at his outrages are as weak and ineffectual as those of Mère Ubu. As grotesquely monstrous as Ubu is, we cannot help recognizing our basic identity with him and admitting that he is merely the exaggeration of our own secret vices and desires. Ubu seems to be aware of this fact; he mocks us while we are mocking him.

Jarry explained his purpose in putting Ubu on stage in "Questions de théâtre":

J'ai voulu que, le rideau levé, la scène fût devant le public comme ce miroir des contes de Mme Leprince de Beaumont, où le vicieux se voit avec des cornes de taureau et un corps de dragon, selon l'exagération de ses vices; et il n'est pas étonnant que le public ait été stupéfait à la vue de son double ignoble, qui ne lui avait pas encore été entièrement présenté; . . . . [23]

Ubu's vices are so exaggerated, he flaunts institutions and authority so brazenly, that audiences were not always able to laugh. As Jarry went on to say in the same article,

. . . l'art et la compréhension de la foule étant si incompatibles, nous aurions si l'on veut eu tort d'attaquer directement la foule dans *Ubu Roi*, elle s'est fâchée parce qu'elle a trop bien compris, quoi qu'elle en dise. [24]

No matter how angry the theater public and some of the critics became, Ubu was there to stay. Rachilde, a close personal and professional friend of Jarry, wrote in her biography of him after his death:

Les critiques impartiaux eurent tout de même, dans ce bouleversant tapage, la vision d'un type nouveau, quoique éternel, de Guignol-tyran, à la fois bour-

---

[22] *Ibid.*

[23] In *Tout Ubu*, p. 140. Mme Jeanne-Marie Leprince de Beaumont (1711-1780) was the author of popular children's stories, among them, *La Belle et la Bête.*

[24] *Ibid.*, p. 141.

geoisement poltron, lâchement cruel, avare, génialement philosophe, tenant par
sa grandiloquence de Shakespeare et par son humanité primitive de Rabelais.

... ...

Ce père Ubu devait, malgré toutes les réprobations et le scandale soulevé,
entrer dans nos mœurs et s'y faire une place qu'on ne peut plus lui enlever.... [25]

In the same work, Rachilde made a statement that is even more true
today than it was then: "Il y a des mythes qui grandissent avec des
époques, et la bêtise du mythe *Ubu* nous écrase à présent de toute sa
sinistre et cynique majesté." [26] The figure of Ubu looms ever larger. In
a world obsessed with violence, a world in which obscenity flourishes,
Ubu is still king.

The second most important character in the play is, of course, Mère
Ubu who is almost a mirror image of her husband: "Madame ma moitié,"
as Ubu aptly calls her. There are, however, a few differences between
them. The major difference is that Mère Ubu does not have the primeval
innocence of her husband. She does indeed share many of his vices, especially greed, but in her they are not so exaggeratedly simple. It is she
who has the original idea of killing the king and usurping the throne.
Unlike Ubu, however, her motivation does not seem to be mere greed;
there is a touch of political ambition and vainglory in it too. She also
seems to be aware, as Ubu is not, that one must play politics in order
to stay in power, even if it means sharing some of the wealth one has
worked so hard to acquire. It is Mère Ubu, along with Bordure, who
persuades Ubu to give the feast for the people. And it is she who wishes
to reward Bordure for his assistance in the conspiracy.

Furthermore, Mère Ubu does seem to recognize some difference between right and wrong and is willing to make at least some concessions
to ethical and social values. It is she who is aware of the threat Bougrelas
poses to them "car il a pour lui le bon droit" (III, i). And she makes a
sincere attempt, although unsuccessful, to persuade Ubu that they should
try to gain his allegiance "par des bienfaits" (III, i).

Mère Ubu also seems to be shocked by Ubu's gratuitous ferocity
— and not just when she is the victim. During the massacre of the nobles,
she exclaims: "De grâce, modère-toi, Père Ubu" (III, ii) and "Quelle
basse férocité" (III, ii).

---

[25] Rachilde, *op. cit.*, pp. 81-82.
[26] *Ibid.*, p. 128.

Let there be no mistake, however; Mère Ubu is not supposed to be seen as being morally superior to her husband. She functions primarily as a foil for Ubu and the differences between them merely emphasize the singular aspects of his character. To use a term from vaudeville, which has comic techniques not entirely different from those found in *Ubu Roi,* Mère Ubu is Ubu's "straight man." How much alike they really are is brought out in the apparition scene. By her treachery, her cowardice, her lies, and her vulgarity, Mère Ubu shows herself to be a worthy match for Ubu. The comedy of character, as well as that of situation and language, reaches one of its peaks in this scene: we have two characters, husband and wife, who are equally vile and who hold each other in the highest contempt, fighting a duel with insults.

One group of characters is very difficult to describe. These are the Palotins, Ubu's henchmen. They were a traditional part of Ubu's entourage from the earliest of the Ubu cycles in Rennes. Their major function was to extract "finance" from Ubu's victims and to carry out his threats. They were very primitive creatures, even more so than Ubu himself, and almost seemed to be some kind of living robots in the manner of Frankenstein. Their original names reflected their crude nature: Mouchedgog, Merdanpot, and Quatrezoneilles. These were the three major Palotins but there seems to have been an army of nameless ones. I have already noted that a stage direction in *Ubu Roi* states: "un palotin explose" (II, ii).

In *Ubu Roi,* the names of the three main Palotins have been changed and their character has been somewhat modified. They are called Giron, Pile, and Cotice, and while at times they do carry out their normal functions as "grippe-sous" and strong men, at other times they seem almost human. On occasion, they even have the intelligence to criticize their master. For example, in IV, i, when Ubu has made a scatological pun, Cotice comments: "Quel pourceau!" And in the following scene, Pile goes so far as to issue an ultimatum to Ubu who, after his cowardly performance during the fight with the bear, orders them to hurry and cook it for his supper: "Ah! c'est trop fort, à la fin! Il faudra travailler ou bien tu n'auras rien, entends-tu, goinfre!" (IV, ii). At the end of the scene, they actually abandon Ubu who has fallen asleep, but a few scenes later, they return to help Ubu escape from Bougrelas and his partisans. Like Mère Ubu, they are really no better than Ubu and are inextricably bound to him to the very end. It is not without reason that they are called "Les Ubs."

The other characters play only minor roles. For the most part, they can be seen as parodies or caricatures of stock types. Not even Bordure, who is the most important of these characters, has any distinguishing characteristics. One might see in him a vague reminiscence of Brutus: he takes part in an assassination conspiracy, later realizes his error, and tries to redeem himself by helping to overthrow the man he has helped to seize power. Further echoes of Shakespeare might also be found in the character of Bougrelas, the young prince who is enjoined by the ghosts of his ancestors to avenge his father's cruel murder. The remaining characters are even more stereotyped: the good but gullible king, the bereaved but noble queen, and the valiant Czar. All of these characters, who are caricatures of heroic figures, serve the same purpose which is the major objective of the play: to put in relief the uniquely monstrous and grotesque figure of Ubu.

LE PARLER UBU

The style or language of *Ubu Roi* is second in importance only to the figure of Ubu himself and is intimately linked to his character; so much so, in fact, that it has been dubbed "le parler Ubu" in Parisian literary circles. This "parler Ubu" is made up of a varied and piquant vocabulary that includes numerous neologisms and archaisms as well as a hearty dose of slang and scatology. It also utilizes the many rhetorical techniques, including the use of repetition, accumulation, exaggeration, puns, platitudes, and jargon, that characterize the style which is most properly called burlesque.

The burlesque style has as its goal to shock the audience into laughter by the combination of the most disparate elements of language and rhetorical patterns. A second, but no less important, purpose is to ridicule the "hero" of the work by putting into his mouth words or expressions that are inappropriate to his station or situation in life. The style of *Ubu Roi*, then, has the important function of adding to the characterization of Ubu and of enhancing the basic parody of plot; but its preponderant function is that of affording a third source of comedy.

Indeed, in certain scenes, the comedy of language seems almost to take precedence, at least momentarily, over the comedy of character and action. At times, the accumulation of techniques of comic style reaches a level of almost pure verbal virtuosity approaching what M. Robert Garapon has called "la fantaisie verbale," which he defines as follows:

... la fantaisie verbale ... constitue un jeu libéré du souci de la signification et placé sous le signe de la gratuité. Pratiquement, il y a fantaisie verbale dès que le plaisir d'assembler les mots et de jouer avec eux prend le pas sur la volonté de signifier.... un texte qui fait la part belle à la fantaisie verbale peut fort bien signifier quelque chose; mais le sens ainsi fourni entre pour bien peu dans l'effet comique produit sur le spectateur. [1]

I will examine examples of "fantaisie verbale" and the comic effect produced by them later in the chapter.

The sound of words plays a major role in the dialogue of the play. It is apparent in the names of the characters, in the words invented or distorted by Jarry, and in the choice of ready-made words or expressions. A comic effect is typically achieved with sounds or combinations of sounds that are generally thought of as ugly, vulgar, or crude.

Several critics have pointed out that the essence of the figure of Ubu is expressed in the name Ubu itself. I have already noted that Jean Morienval, who considers the choice of a suitable name to be one of the basic requirements for the creation of a true comic type, finds the name Ubu to be a particularly felicitous invention. The repetition of the single vowel "u," the explosion of the consonant, and the brevity of the word create an impression of ridiculousness. The very sound of the name thus conveys the grotesqueness of the character to whom it belongs.

It is interesting to speculate on how Jarry arrived at the name Ubu. In typical schoolboy slang, Hébert was modified into Hébé, supposedly in imitation of Hébert's own pronunciation of his name. According to Henri Morin, when Jarry left for Paris taking *Les Polonais* with him, he obtained permission from Morin to make whatever use of the schoolboy farce that he might on the condition that he change the name of the major character from Hébé or Père Heb to something less recognizable. [2] Whether Morin's version of the story is true or whether Jarry would have changed the name without Morin's insistence is impossible to know and is actually unimportant. What is important is that Jarry did rechristen Hébé Ubu and in so doing immortalized him.

J. H. Sainmont has suggested that Jarry chose the vowel "u" in order to create an internal rhyme in the chorus line of the "Chanson du décervelage":

---

[1] Robert Garapon, *La Fantaisie verbale et le comique dans le théâtre français du moyen âge jusqu'à la fin du XVIIe siècle* (Paris: Librairie Armand Colin, 1957), p. 10.

[2] See Chassé, *op. cit.*, p. 55.

Hourra, cornes-au-cul, vive le Père *Ubu*. [3]

Jarry himself commented on the name Ubu in his article "Les Paralipo-mènes d'Ubu," but, in his typically mystifying manner, he did not tell us exactly how he arrived at the name:

Je ne sais pas ce que veut dire le nom d'Ubu, qui est la déformation en plus éternel du nom de son accidentel prototype encore vivant; *Ybex* peut-être, le Vautour. [4]

Later in the same article, Jarry compared Ubu to "la bête marine la plus esthétiquement horrible, la limule." In his article on "Le Vocabu-laire d'Alfred Jarry," A. Carey Taylor says that Jarry's emphasis on words like *Ybex* and *limule* suggests that

Jarry tendait à croire que la voyelle *u* (qui se trouve, par exemple, dans le verbe *huer*) était mieux faite que toute autre pour exprimer ce qu'il y a de méprisable dans le veule personnage auquel il donnait sa forme définitive. [5]

The addition of the popular form of address, Père, to the name Ubu heightens the impression of vulgarity. The name Mère Ubu is an echo of Père Ubu and points out the basic similarity between the two char-acters. The title of the play, in which the ridiculous name Ubu is juxta-posed with the grandiose title Roi, gives an indication of the enormous parody that the play contains.

The most important character after Père and Mère Ubu is Capitaine Bordure, their fellow conspirator who betrays them. The name Bordure, like the name Ubu, was invented by Jarry alone after he had taken the play to Paris. "Bordure" is a term in heraldry in which Jarry was quite interested and well versed. He and Rémy de Gourmont made extensive use of heraldic figures and terms in the short-lived art review, *L'Ymagier,* of which they were co-founders and co-editors. Heraldry was also a dom-inant theme of *César-Antéchrist,* published in 1895, in which "l'Acte Terrestre" consisted of a shortened and slightly modified version of *Ubu Roi.* It was perhaps at this time that Jarry chose the name Bordure as

---

[3] Sainmont, "Ubu ou la création d'un mythe,» *Cahiers du Collège de 'Pata-physique,* No. 3-4, (1951), 57-69.

[4] In *Tout Ubu,* p. 151.

[5] *C.A.I.E.F.,* 11 (May, 1959), 314.

well as the names of the three Palotins which are also names of heraldic figures. But the sound of the names seems of far greater significance than their heraldic meaning.

In the name Bordure we find again a combination of vowels and consonants that produces a vulgar or crude sound. In particular the *r* sound which ends each syllable creates an impression of harshness. Mr. Taylor also notes in his article: "Nous sommes tentés de croire que la rime riche que ce mot fait avec *ordure* n'est pas une simple coïncidence." [6]

Giron, Pile, and Cotice are the names of the three Palotins, Ubu's unusual henchmen. Mr. Taylor suggests that the name Palotin itself came from the "perhébertique" legend of Rennes and that it was "un croisement amusant de *paladin, palatin,* et *salopin.*" [7] One might also mention that the "supplice du pal," which figures prominently in *Ubu Cocu* was one of Ubu's favorite tortures and was frequently carried out by the Palotins. Thus their title might also be indicative of their function. Giron, Pile, and Cotice sound more like the names of objects than of people and are therefore quite appropriate for the mechanical puppets they adorn.

Another picturesque group of names consists of those which have a Slavic sound. The play is supposedly set in Poland and it retains as its subtitle the original title of *Les Polonais.* The most important of these Polish names are those of the king, Venceslas, and his three sons, Boleslas, Ladislas, and Bougrelas. All but the last of these were common names of the kings of Bohemia and Poland. Jarry comments on this fact in his written presentation of the play that was distributed to the audience at the Théâtre de l'Œuvre:

> Fort tard après la pièce écrite, on s'est aperçu qu'il y avait eu en des temps anciens, au pays où fut premier roi Pyast, homme rustique, un certain Rogatka ou Henry au grand ventre, qui succéda à un roi Venceslas, et aux trois fils dudit, Boleslas et Ladislas, le troisième n'étant pas Bougrelas; et que ce Venceslas, ou un autre, fut dit l'Ivrogne. Nous ne trouvons pas honorable de construire des pièces historiques. [8]

Again, the sound of the names seems to be of primary importance rather than any specific historical reference. Their foreign sound would auto-

---

[6] *Ibid.,* p. 318.

[7] *Ibid.,* p. 315.

[8] Quoted in *Tout Ubu,* p. 21.

matically seem comic to French ears. And once more we notice the repetition of sounds in all four names which increases the comic effect. The
most important character of the four is Bougrelas and his is the most
unusual of the four names. It is nothing more than a derogatory epithet
with the Slavic-sounding ending -las. A hero with such a name could not
possibly be taken seriously, just as no audience could sympathize with a
character named Bordure.

The other characters with Polish-sounding names play only minor
roles in the play. Some of these names were also drawn from history
books, but their historical connotation is even less meaningful than in the
names just discussed. For example, Stanislas Leczinski, the name of
the peasant from whom Ubu tries to collect taxes in III, iv, was the king
of Poland in the first half of the eighteenth century and was also ruler of
the duchies of Bar and Lorraine. His daughter, Marie, married the king
of France, Louis XV. Jean Sobiesky, also king of Poland from 1673-1696
and a Polish national hero, is the name of one of Ubu's soldiers killed
in the battle with the Russians. The other characters with Slavic names
include Michel Fédérovitch who wins the footrace in II, vii; Nicholas
Rensky, a young soldier who brings Ubu the message of the Polish
uprising against him and who is also killed in the battle with the Russians; and Général Lascy, [9] the commander of Ubu's army. All of these
characters might have had larger roles in earlier versions of the play or
in other parts of the Ubu cycle. In fact, their roles in *Ubu Roi* hardly
qualify them to be given a name at all. They do add to the Slavic flavor
of the play, however.

An even more important group of words in which sound is an especially essential element is that which includes words distorted or invented
by Jarry. One word in particular stands out, the very first word of the
play which caused such a furor on the night of December 10, 1896
— "merdre." The slight distortion of the still recognizable word seems
somehow to have increased rather than diminished its effect. From all
indications, this form dates from the earliest of the Ubu cycles in Rennes
and is a typical example of schoolboy slang with its combination of scatology and the playful distortion of the sounds of words. Charles Morin
gives an interesting and relatively probable account of the origin of the

---

[9] Perhaps this name is an allusion to the Polish military hero, Laski.

form *merdre*. [10] A. Carey Taylor suggests that the choice of the consonant *r* was probably based on a popular paronomasia as in the pronunciation of *robre* for *robe,* common in lower-class Parisian speech. Mr. Taylor adds:

La terminaison -rdre lui donne une sonorité et une truculence qui ont dû faire la joie des potaches du lycée de Rennes à qui Jarry l'a sans doute emprunté. [11]

Like *merdre,* many of the other neologisms found in the play were part of the special argot created by the students of the Lycée de Rennes to be used in the many spoofs of their unfortunate physics professor. Some were simple distortions of common words by the addition or interpolation of a single letter as in the form *oneille* for *oreille* or *tuder* for *tuer.* Other creations were more complex and the origin of these forms is often difficult if not impossible to determine. Charles Morin has offered an ingenious explanation of the etymology of the word *rastron* which occurs in the burlesque dinner scene in I, iii. [12] The *côtes de rastron* were part of the bizarre menu prepared by Mère Ubu. Jarry himself, however, gives a different explanation, albeit a fictional one, of the origin of the same word in his novel *L'Amour absolu. Rastron* was one of the names which Emmanuel, the main character in the novel, gave to the animals in his Noah's Ark when he was a child: "*Rahirs* et *rastrons* furent les plus beaux, dont Emmanuel lui-même oublia le sens. . . ." [13] The origin of the word, however, is not as important as the particular use made of it in the play, and here again we must look to the sound of the word in order to determine the nature of the effect produced. Essentially it is the word *rat* with a suffix *-stron* whose combination of consonants and the nasal *on* serve to inflate the word and give it a crudely comical sound. From the sound of the word, then, we imagine a *rastron* to be a large and comical rodentlike animal. [14] And *côtes de rastron* seem as grotesque and whimsical as grasshoppers' knees or toads' toes.

A very important group of neologisms the etymology of which is also difficult to determine is the group of terms used to describe Ubu's most

---

[10] See above, p. 36.

[11] Taylor, *op. cit.,* p. 307.

[12] See above, p. 37.

[13] In *Œuvres complètes,* I, 58.

[14] We might note that Robert does list the word "raton" as a diminutive of the word "rat."

conspicuous physical characteristic and the one which becomes, as I have already mentioned, the symbol of his entire nature, that is his *gidouille, boudouille,* or *giborgne* as it is alternately called. *Gidouille* and *boudouille* are possibly distortions of *andouille* with which they share a basic similarity of sound and meaning. *Giborgne* is a further variation on the same theme. The word *borgne* means basically "having only one eye" and by extension "having a single orifice," thus possibly suggesting Ubu's umbilicus. *Borgne* has a figurative derogatory meaning as well, as in the expressions *maison borgne* and *cabaret borgne.* In all three cases, the sound of the word perfectly suggests the grotesqueness of the thing it designates. A fourth term, *bouzine,* is used to name the same object in I, iv. Mr. Taylor suggests that Jarry might have drawn this word from Rabelais. According to Mr. Taylor, Rabelais "employait ce mot dans le sens de *cornemuse,* instrument dont la forme rappelle suffisament la *gidouille* d'Ubu." [15] Jarry may too have been thinking of a vulgar but popular word, *bouse.* I might add that the word *bouzine* has the same expressivity that is found in *gidouille, boudouille,* and *giborgne.*

Since Ubu was modeled on a professor of physics and since greed is his major vice, it is understandable that the words *finances* and *physique* should take on a special significance in the play. They, like *merdre* and the various forms of *gidouille,* function as leitmotifs that recur throughout the play. *Finances* is sometimes written *phynances* as in *Le Théâtre des Phynances,* the name given to the attic in Rennes where *Ubu* received its first performances. Taylor suggests that this spelling, like the term *bouzine,* was based on the high-school students' study of Rabelais and other writers of the Renaissance.

It is true that several other archaisms or pseudo-archaisms are found in the play: *estes* (I, i and vi); *Monsieuye* (IV, v and vi); *par conséiquent de quoye* (IV, v and V, vii); *ji tou tue* (III, viii); *ji lon mets dans ma poche* (IV, vii); and *ji lon fous à la poche* (IV, v). In some cases, only the spelling is archaic and does not influence the sound of the word so that its impact on a theater audience is lessened, whereas for a reader of the play the word stands out in relief. In other cases, however, the spelling does influence the sound, and, as is true with the neologisms, the peculiarity or oddity of the sound gives it an essentially comic

---

[15] Taylor, *op. cit.,* p. 307.

effect, especially in the case of the threats *ji tou tue* and *ji lon fous à la poche.*

In the case of *finances* and *physique,* it is not so much the sound of the words as the particular use made of them which is important. Almost as soon as he has become king, Ubu kills the Ministers of Finance and appoints himself *Maître des Finances.* This title is much more valid than the title *Roi* both as a symbol of his greed and as a description of his actions. Mère Ubu quite logically becomes *Madame la financière* (III, vii). Mr. Taylor points out that

> Le terme *Maître des Finances* devient bientôt le titre officiel par excellence de l'usurpateur, comme les titres de *Führer* ou de *Duce* plus tard, et l'expression *à finances* prend le sens de "royal" ou d'"Officiel"....[16]

As Ubu sets out to collect taxes from village to village, he takes with him the *voiturin à phynances* and the *salopins de finance* (III, iv). Later when he goes off to war, he rides the *cheval à phynance,* wears a *casque à finances,* arms himself with a *croc à finances* and a *pistolet à phynances.* And, during the pause before the battle with the Russians, Ubu asks his soldiers to sing the *Chanson à Finances,* obviously the ubuesque equivalent of "God Save the King."

Finance or *phynance* is also the term used to designate any kind of money or wealth. When Ubu goes around collecting taxes, he commands his subjects to produce their *finance* and not their *argent.* In giving a "financial," in its double meaning, report to his advisors, he speaks of "des gens pliant sous le poids de nos phynances" (III, vii). Later in the same scene, when Ubu learns that Bordure and the Czar have joined forces to defeat him, he attempts to bribe the saints to help him with offers of *phynance*: "Saint Antoine et tous les saints, protégez-moi, je vous donnerai de la phynance et je brûlerai des cierges pour vous" (III, vii).

One of Ubu's distinguishing characteristics is his constant and almost virtuoso use of interjections and curses. *Merdre* is, of course, Ubu's trademark. It occurs a total of thirty-three times in the course of the play. It is most commonly used as a simple curse, but it is also used in numerous other ways and in combination with other words. As an expletive or curse, we find several different combinations: *Bougre de merdre,*

---

[16] *Ibid.,* p. 312.

merdre de bougre (I, i), and *de par ma merdre* (III, iii) which echo
another of Ubu's favorite exclamations, *de par ma chandelle verte. Merdre*
is also quite naturally used as the signal to begin the attack on the king.
And it is occasionally used as a derogatory epithet, as when Mère Ubu
calls Père Ubu *grosse merdre* (I, iv). Or, in some cases, it can almost
become a gruff term of kinship or affection, as when Ubu calls his wife
Madame de ma merdre (III, vii) or when he calls Nicholas Rensky
Garçon de ma merdre (IV, iii). And like *finances* and *physique, merdre*
sometimes takes on the meaning of "royal" or "official." Thus Ubu's arms
are sometimes called *sabre à merdre, croc à merdre,* or *ciseau à merdre*
just as they are called *croc à finances, bâton à physique,* etc.

Like *merdre*, other favorite curses or interjections of Ubu were drawn
from the special argot of the Ubu cycle in Rennes. I have already mentioned that one of his favorite exclamations is *de par ma chandelle verte.*
According to Henri Morin, this expression originated in one of the earlier
plays in the Ubu cycle in which a green candle was used by Ubu as a
signal to his men when they were to go out on a midnight raid. Similarly
la poche which figures in a variety of ingenious threats in the play, for
example "je te poche avec décollation et torsion des jambes" (III, vii)
and "ji lon mets dans ma poche avec torsion du nez et des dents et
extraction de la langue" (III, vii), was originally a large *sac* which Ubu
dragged along behind him and into which he stuffed all the *phynance*
he was able to steal or otherwise acquire. Whatever the origin of the
expressions, they add a note of colorful fantasy to Ubu's curses and
threats.

Ubu also frequently swears upon his *gidouille* to which he often adds
the word *corne* as a prefix. This term was part of another leitmotif in the
geste d'Ubu which is prominent in *Ubu Cocu* and that is the cuckolding
of Père Ubu. This leitmotif is only briefly touched upon in *Ubu Roi* in
the hints or suggestions of a liaison between Mère Ubu and the Palotin
Giron while Ubu is off at war. Nevertheless, the term *corne* remains one
of the basic elements of Ubu's repertory of curses. Sometimes it is used
as a separate word as in the expressions *corne de ma gidouille, corne
finances, corne physique,* and *corne d'Ubu.* At other times, it is joined
to the other terms so that the two become one word, as in the forms
cornegidouille, cornefinance, and *cornebleu.* In these examples, we also
notice that *finance* and *physique* figure prominently in Ubu's repertory

of interjections. One might say that he swears upon everything that is dear to him.

Other fanciful exclamations include *tête de vache, sac à vin, ventre-bleu,* and *jambedieu.* Ubu does not hesitate to use ready-made interjections. Some are traditional euphemisms which have a colloquial flavor, such as *jarnicotonbleu* and *sapristi.* We also occasionally find a simple *Seigneur* or *Dieu.* But of course Ubu's favorite of the ready-made curses is also the most vulgar, that is *bougre.* He puts it to a variety of uses just as he does with all of his favorite words. He uses it as an epithet: "Il n'est pas bête, le bougre, il a deviné" (I, iv), and as an exclamation, "Bougre, que c'est mauvais!" (I, iii).

It seems quite natural and in perfect accordance with Ubu's use of his own special argot and with his fondness for curses and vulgarity that his vocabulary should also include a number of slang or colloquial expressions. They have several important characteristics in common with the expressions discussed up to now. Their very sound usually conveys an impression of crude humor and they add to the characterization of Ubu by emphasizing his basic vulgarity. A typical example and one of the most frequently used is the term *bouffre* which means basically "glutton" and, by extension, "greedy person." It retains this meaning in the following instances. When Ubu is protesting against the custom of giving a feast for the people to celebrate his succession to the throne, he refers to his subjects as *ces bouffres*: "Voulez-vous me ruiner pour ces bouf-fres?" (I, vi). Similarly, when Ubu tells Mère Ubu that he has no intention of giving Bordure the duchy that he has promised him, he refers to him as *ce bouffre* (III, i). At other times, however, the term seems to be used as a general term of scorn, as when Ubu calls the nobles *bouffres.* Ubu also creates a feminine form of the word, *bouffresque,* that he uses for Mère Ubu (III, ii and vii).

Another of Ubu's favorite insults, also part of the same leitmotif of gluttony, is *andouille,* a term which he uses for Mère Ubu on several occasions, for example in I, v, and twice in the apparition scene in V, i. Also found in the latter scene is the even more deprecatory *charogne.* The names that Ubu is called by other people are no less colorful. The people closest to him and who know him the best are the ones who use the most insulting epithets. His fellow conspirators call him *traître et gueux voyou* (I, iii), and Pile calls him *révoltante bourrique* and *goinfre* (IV, vi). *Bourrique* is also one of Mère Ubu's favorite terms for her husband.

Ubu uses numerous other slang expressions besides those used as insults. For example, we find *foutre le camp* and *filer* for "to go away," *binette* and *fiole* for "head," *flingot* for "gun," and *rond* for "drunk."

Ubu's use of slang and colloquial expressions is another aspect of his frequent use of language inappropriate to the traditional situation which is being parodied. This language can therefore be categorized as part of the basic burlesque that functions in every element of the structure of the play: plot, characterization, and dialogue. This is particularly apparent in certain examples. The burlesque tone is set in the very first scene of the play by the language Mère Ubu uses in persuading Ubu to kill the king and usurp the throne. For example, she says:

... vous vous contentez de mener aux revues une cinquantaine d'estafiers armés de coupe-choux, quand vous pourriez faire succéder sur votre fiole la couronne de Pologne à celle d'Aragon? (I, i)

Later in the scene, Ubu introduces an even more vulgar note into the discussion: "Et vraiment! et puis après? N'ai-je pas un cul comme les autres?" (I, i). Mère Ubu picks it up and cleverly fits it into her argument:

A ta place, ce cul, je voudrais l'installer sur un trône. Tu pourrais augmenter indéfiniment tes richesses, manger fort souvent de l'andouille et rouler carosse par les rues. (I, i)

I have already mentioned Ubu's use of crude language in his interview with the king. [17] In the scene following, in which the conspirators make their final plans for the assassination, Ubu also uses several familiar or colloquial terms. His first suggestion as a method for killing the king is "d'empoisonner simplement le roi en lui fourrant de l'arsenic dans son déjeuner. Quand il voudra le brouter, il tombera mort et ainsi je serai roi" (I, vii). In this scene as in the preceding one, the crudeness of the language has a function similar to that of the slapstick at the conspirators' dinner: it eliminates any seriousness from the scene and contributes to the basic parody of plot as well as adding to the characterization of Ubu. None of the other characters uses much more elevated language than Ubu, however. For instance, Bordure's first suggestion as to how to kill the king also includes slang: "Moi, je suis d'avis de lui ficher un grand coup d'épée qui le fendra de la tête à la ceinture" (I, vii). Everyone, except

---

[17] See above, p. 65.

Ubu, seems to think that this is a more noble way of killing the king. This is the occasion when Ubu declares that he would betray them if he thought that there was any danger: "... je filerais vous dénoncer pour me tirer de cette sale affaire..." (I, vii). This statement provokes a volley of insults from Mère Ubu who is almost as adept as her husband at name calling: "Oh! le traître, le lâche, le vilain et plat ladre" (I, vii). But Ubu finally is persuaded to stay with the conspirators, and Bordure then suggests another manner of carrying out their plan. As before, the use of slang completely degrades the action he is proposing and puts it in the realm of comic fantasy: "Ne vaudrait-il pas mieux nous jeter tous à la fois sur lui en braillant et gueulant? Nous aurions chance ainsi d'entraîner les troupes" (I, vii). Ubu agrees to this proposal and adds an even more ludicrous suggestion:

Alors voilà. Je tâcherai de lui marcher sur les pieds, il regimbera, alors je lui dirai: MERDRE, et à ce signal vous vous jetterez sur lui. (I, vii)

After Ubu has become king, his first comment on his new condition shows immediately that there is to be no improvement in his language or his mentality: "De par ma chandelle verte, me voici roi de ce pays, je me suis déjà flanqué une indigestion et on va m'apporter ma grande capeline" (III, i). It is in this same scene that Mère Ubu mentions their debt to Bordure and Ubu scornfully replies:

De grâce, Mère Ubu, ne me parle pas de ce bouffre. Maintenant que je n'ai plus besoin de lui, il peut bien se brosser le ventre, il n'aura pas son duché. (III, i)

Later in the scene when Mère Ubu mentions Bougrelas, Ubu replies with similar language that reflects a similar attitude: "Que veux-tu qu'il me fasse, ce petit gamin de quatorze ans?" (III, i). Mère Ubu then counters with an equally colloquial warning: "Fais à ta tête, Père Ubu, il t'en cuira" (III, i).

Another scene in which Ubu uses numerous slang or vulgar words and expressions is the scene in which he condemns the nobles to death and throws them through the trapdoor that leads to the basement where they undergo Ubu's favorite form of execution, le décervelage. Ubu's use of slang and vulgarity at this point has several functions. It demonstrates his total lack of respect and concern for the persons he is condemning to death out of pure greed and it reflects his obscene enjoyment of his own brutality. And, as in preceding scenes, it removes the episode from the realm of reality through the grotesque exaggeration of dialogue that parallels the exaggeration of situation and action.

Ubu addresses each of the nobles with the familiar *tu* and calls them *bouffre* throughout the scene. He further insults one of them by saying "Tu as une sale tête" (III, ii). When he is pleased with the title or possessions they have to offer, he expresses his satisfaction with a colloquialism: "Excellent! excellent! Je n'en demande pas plus long. Dans la trappe" (III, ii). And he expresses his disappointment with yet another colloquial expression: "Ça n'est pas lourd. Tu n'as rien autre chose?" (III, ii).

There are other expressions which, if not actually slang, have a definitely colloquial ring to them. To cite a case in point, in the scene in which the assassination takes place, the king calls Ubu to him with very elegant language: "Noble Père Ubu, venez près de moi avec votre suite pour inspecter les troupes" (II, ii), to which Ubu responds with the familiar sounding: "On y va, monsieur, on y va" (II, ii). Later when Mère Ubu and the *Conseillers de Phynances* are trying to persuade him to go to war to defend himself against the Russians, Ubu answers: "Ah! non, par exemple.... Je ne veux pas donner d'argent. En voilà d'une autre" (III, vi).

Another habit of speech which gives Ubu's language a colloquial flavor is the use of proverbs or platitudes. The first proverbial expression occurs in the opening scene when Mère Ubu is trying to persuade Ubu to kill the king. Ubu states: "Ventrebleu, de par ma chandelle verte, j'aime mieux être gueux comme un maigre et brave rat que riche comme un méchant et gras chat" (I, i). The sentiment that he is expressing here is quite uncharacteristic. We must assume that he is not really sincere in making such a statement, but is merely trying to cover up his cowardice. The language, on the other hand, is quite typical of him and is in direct contrast to the noble sentiment expressed. The humor of his statement arises from the colorful imagery, the clever balance in meaning and sound between the two antithetical terms, and the double contrast between expression and meaning and between what Ubu says and what he actually feels.

The other proverbs or proverbial expressions in the play produce a different comic effect and one that is more in line with the basic burlesque aspect. They are amusing or comic primarily because of their incongruity or inappropriateness to the situation. A typical example occurs in I, iv. Ubu and Capitaine Bordure are commenting on the dinner. Bordure states that he did not particularly enjoy *la merdre,* Ubu says that he did, and Mère Ubu makes the trite observation: "Chacun son goût" (I, iv), which is especially comical in this case because of its application to such an unusual subject. The omission of "à" adds to the popular flavor.

A similar example occurs in II, ii, the scene in which Ubu condemns the nobles and throws them through the trap in order to seize their titles and possessions. When the fifth noble names his rather unimpressive possessions, Ubu philosophically replies: "Eh bien, mieux vaut peu que rien. Dans la trappe" (III, ii). Here again, the humor arises from the contrast between the use of a common, everyday expression and the unusual and grotesque situation in which it is used.

Another proverbial expression occurs in II, iv. In this case, the comedy arises from an effect of exaggeration. Père Ubu has come to collect taxes from the peasants. He enters the peasants' house and demands to speak to the oldest man present. As soon as Stanislas Leczinski steps forward, Ubu begins to scream at him to listen. When Leczinski calmly replies that Ubu has not said anything yet, Ubu retorts: "Comment, je parle depuis une heure. Crois-tu que je vienne ici pour prêcher dans le désert?" (III, iv). The dialogue has reached an advanced level of the burlesque at this point in the play.

I have already alluded to Ubu's crude form of humor which is present, for example, in his use of slang and platitudes in the scene with the nobles. The same kind of humor is present in several other instances. The witticisms are often based on a sudden turn or reversal of thought or on pure nonsense. In I, ii, when Père and Mère Ubu are waiting for their dinner guests, Ubu makes the unexpected pronouncement: "Mère Ubu, tu es bien laide aujourd'hui. Est-ce parce que nous avons du monde?" In another example, the joke is on Ubu when he tells Mère Ubu: "Sabre à finances, corne de ma gidouille, j'ai des oneilles pour parler et vous une bouche pour m'entendre" (III, vii). When his followers burst out laughing, he realizes his error, but in trying to correct his mistake he merely compounds it. "Ou plutôt non! Vous me faites tromper et vous êtes cause que je suis bête!" (III, vii). I have already quoted the vulgar pun Ubu makes on the word *fuite* after the battle with the Russians. [18] In the same scene, when he is bragging about his non-existent courage during the battle, he boasts: "Moi, j'ai déployé la plus grande valeur, et sans m'exposer j'ai massacré quatre ennemis de ma propre main, sans compter tous ceux qui étaient morts et que nous avons achevés" (IV, v).

Several critics attacked the play for the banality, if not absurdity, of the puns and witticisms. Jarry himself answered this criticism in his article "Questions de théâtre."

Vraiment, il n'y a pas de quoi attendre une pièce drôle, et les masques expliquent que le comique doit en être tout au plus le comique macabre d'un clown anglais ou d'une danse des morts. ... Et surtout on n'a pas compris — ce qui était pourtant assez clair et rappelé perpetuellement par les répliques de la Mère Ubu: "Quel sot homme! ... quel triste imbécile," — qu'Ubu ne devait pas dire "des mots d'esprit" comme divers ubucules en réclamaient, mais des phrases stupides, avec toute l'autorité du Mufle. [19]

The primary function of these puns and witticisms, then, is to add to the characterization of Ubu. The humor comes not so much from the puns themselves as from their incongruity or absurdity which serves to demonstrate Ubu's stupidity.

The picturesque quality of Ubu's language is increased by the number of concrete images he uses, especially in his threats, his complaints, and his expressions of fear. The threats are characterized by cruel violence. I have already mentioned the particularly graphic list of tortures which comprise what Ubu calls *le dernier supplice* with which he threatens Mère Ubu during the apparition scene in V, i. There are numerous variations of this threat which occur throughout the play. For example, when Ubu is attempting to extract money from the peasants, he typically does so with a threat: "Payez, ou je vous mets dans ma poche avec supplice et décollation du cou et de la tête!" (III, iv). A few scenes later, Ubu greets a messenger with: "Va-t-en, sagouin, ou je te poche avec décollation et torsion des jambes" (III, vii). And Ubu goes off to war, chanting "Torsion du nez et des dents, extraction de la langue et enfoncement du petit bout de bois dans les oneilles" (III, viii).

I have also mentioned the frequency with which Ubu threatens Mère Ubu, sometimes with *le dernier supplice,* as in the aforementioned instance

---

[18] See above, p. 64.
[19] In *Tout Ubu,* p. 140.

and, at other times, with tortures that he invents at the moment but which are no less graphic or colorful. Here are several examples: "Vous allez passer tout à l'heure par la casserole" (I, i); "Je te vais arracher les yeux" (I, ii); "Je vais aiguiser mes dents contre vos mollets" (I, iii); "Je vais te marcher sur les pieds" (I, iv); "Je vais te mettre en morceaux" (III, ii).

Ubu's complaints and expressions of fear contain terms that are equally concrete and equally ingenious. In the scene in which they plan the assassination, Ubu expresses his fear of the king in this manner: "Et s'il vous donne des coups de pied? Je me rappelle maintenant qu'il a pour les revues des souliers de fer qui font très mal" (I, viii). The incongruity of the statement heightens the comic effect. This is true of a similar statement made by Ubu in the midst of the battle with the Russians: "Je n'en peux plus, je suis criblé de coups de pied, je voudrais m'asseoir par terre" (IV, iv). Ubu's loud complaints when he falls during his interview with the king in I, vi, belong in the same category.

The list of Ubu's arms is also part of the vocabulary of violence that is one of the dominant themes of the play. The list is quite long, and if Ubu wore or carried all these arms at once, he must indeed have presented quite a grotesque figure. The more common or usual weapons include *un sabre, un pistolet,* and *un couteau.* Somewhat less common are *le croc* or *le crochet, le bâton,* and *le ciseau.* The most unique of all is *le petit bout de bois* which Ubu drives into his victims' ears. As I have mentioned earlier, the names of these weapons are often supplemented by the words *à merdre, à phynances,* or *à physique* which are part of Ubu's royal emblem. The addition of these words also serves to remove the objects from the realm of reality. Other phrases are sometimes used which describe the function or purpose of the arm such as *le couteau à figure* and *le ciseau à oneilles.* Even *le croc à finance* has a certain descriptive value. The primitivism of the weapons and the echo of childish brutality of their very names suggest that they were part of the Ubu cycle at the Lycée de Rennes along with *la poche* and *le dernier supplice.*

But in addition to being a greedy, crude, obscene, brutal coward, Ubu also has certain pretensions which are reflected in his language. At times he will use words or phrases that are quite elaborate and elegant. These form a sharp contrast to the colloquial or vulgar expressions that continue to flow from his lips and heighten the overall impression of incongruity. Roger Shattuck observes in *The Banquet Years*: "The pompous manner of address inflates and deflates itself as it goes along."[20] For example, Ubu frequently alternates between the royal *nous* and the simple *je* in the same speech.

Ubu's pretensions are apparent in the rather fanciful titles which he assumes and which he confers on all those around him. *Maître des Finances,* which I have already discussed, is his main title. It is sometimes varied by substituting *Monsieuye* for *Maître*. We also find simply *Monsieuye Ubu* (IV, v and vi), an occasional *Seigneur Ubu* (III, vii), and several examples of *Sire Ubu* (IV, iii and iv, and V, ii). The most fanciful but not always flattering appelations are those which Ubu uses for Mère Ubu: "Madame ma femelle" (III, i), "Madame ma moitié" (V, ii), "Madame de ma merdre" (III, vii), and "Madame la financière" (III, vii). When Mère Ubu is posing as the Archangel Gabriel, Ubu gives her the fitting title "Madame l'Apparition" (V, ii).

Similarly, Ubu creates new titles for his henchmen, the Palotins. When they are assisting him in the collection of taxes, he gives them the formal title "messeigneurs les salopins de finance" (III, iv) which is sometimes shortened to "Messieurs des Finances" (III, iv, and V, ii). Their fealty to their master is indicated in the less grandiose title "Les Père Ubus" (V, ii) or simply "les Ubs" (V, ii and iii). Ubu even calls his horse "monsieur notre cheval à finances" (IV, iv) and addresses the boat as "Monsieur l'Equipage" (V, iv). He also occasionally shows an exaggerated politeness to his soldiers whom he addresses in terms of medieval chivalry: "Sire Soldat" and "Sire Lancier" (IV, iii). The entire speech is worth quoting because it is a model of comic pretentiousness.

Cornebleu, jambedieu, tête de vache! Nous allons périr, car nous mourons de soif et sommes fatigué. Sire Soldat, ayez l'obligeance de porter notre casque à finances, et vous, sire Lancier, chargez-vous du ciseau à merdre et du bâton à physique pour soulager notre personne, car, je le répète, nous sommes fatigué. (IV, iii)

Here again, Ubu uses burlesque language which clashes with the situation, but, in this instance, Ubu has gone to the opposite extreme from his normal vulgarity.

Quite often, not only is the pretentiousness of the language inappropriate, but the words are also used incorrectly or are deflected from their

---

[20] P. 179.

usual meaning or usage. This is particularly true in speeches in which Ubu uses three or four words with the same meaning for emphasis. For example, when he is collecting taxes from the peasants, he announces: "Je viens donc te dire, t'ordonner et te signifier que tu aies à produire et exhiber promptement ta finance, sinon tu seras massacré" (III, iv). [21] And in the speech in which he exhorts his arms to kill the Czar, he tells *le petit bout de bois* to "massacrer, creuser et exploiter l'Empereur moscovite" (IV, iv). Later in the same scene, when he and his men have been put to flight, he threatens one of his own soldiers: "Fais attention ou tu vas expérimenter la bouillante valeur du Maître des Phynances" (IV, iv).

It is apparent from some of these examples that Ubu's verbal pretensions slip easily into the exaggerated and pompous speech, called *rodomontade,* which is often associated with similar comic types such as *le matamore* or the pedant. This type of speech is frequently characterized by *la fantaisie verbale* in which verbal play or virtuosity take precedence over meaning or signification. The *fantaisie verbale* present in Ubu's speeches has a double function: to emphasize Ubu's pretensions and stupidity through the use of language that tends toward absurdity or meaninglessness, and, secondly, to provoke laughter by pure verbal virtuosity. We laugh at Ubu for his *bêtise,* but at the same time we admire his cleverness with words and we are caught up with him in a feeling of intoxication that is produced by this kind of verbal play. The basic techniques used to create this impression of *fantaisie verbale* are repetition, enumeration, and the use of jargon which includes the neologisms and argot already discussed as well as technical terms and Latin.

The most obvious and frequent cases of repetition and accumulation are Ubu's exclamations. He seldom opens his mouth without using several of his favorite oaths. A typical example is in III, iii, when Ubu knocks at the door of a peasant and demands: "Cornegidouille! Ouvrez, de par ma merdre, par saint Jean, saint Pierre et saint Nicholas! ouvrez, sabre à finances, corne finances, je viens chercher les impôts!" The speech just quoted from the following scene where he demands their money also includes repetition and enumeration. It concludes: "Allons, messeigneurs les salopins de finance, voiturez ici le voiturin à phynances" (III, iv).

---

[21] This is reminiscent of a similar stylistic formula used by Rabelais. See, for example, the Prologue to *Pantagruel.*

A particularly amusing use of repetition, both from the point of view of its characterization of Ubu and of its pure verbal virtuosity, is found in the battle scene. A Russian soldier fires a pistol at Ubu who, not waiting to determine whether or not he has been hit, bursts out in a crescendo series of exclamations, "Ah! Oh! Je suis blessé, je suis troué, je suis perforé, je suis administré, je suis enterré" (IV, iv). Later in this scene, we find a similar example in which parody of the pompous language of officialdom helps to create an effect of comic fantasy. This is the speech in which Ubu addresses his weapons as if they had powers of their own:

Que le bâton à physique travaille d'une généreuse émulation et partage avec le petit bout de bois l'honneur de massacrer, creuser et exploiter l'Empereur moscovite. . . . (IV, iv)

The most extreme case of repetition occurs in the scene immediately following the battle. It has just been learned that Nicholas Rensky was killed during the battle, and Ubu delivers a burlesque eulogy for him which takes a common metaphor and turns it into a grotesque joke through the gratuitous repetition and variation of two words:

Ainsi que le coquelicot et le pissenlit à la fleur de leur âge sont fauchés par l'impitoyable faucheur qui fauche impitoyablement leur pitoyable binette, ainsi le petit Rensky a fait le coquelicot, il s'est fort bien battu cependant, mais aussi, il y avait trop de Russes. (IV, v)

The final descent to the trite popular syntax of the "mais aussi . . . " accentuates the parody.

There are several kinds of enumeration found in *Ubu Roi* besides the examples already mentioned. The first of these is the exotic list of foods that comprise the menu for the conspirators' dinner. [22] Another type that occurs is the enumeration of insults. Repetition of sound also plays a role in this kind of enumeration. The first example occurs in Act II during the fight between Bougrelas and Ubu and his men, a fight from which Bougrelas emerges victorious. The sound of these insults creates a comic effect that complements the burlesque action which is taking place: "Chenapans, sacs à vin, sagouins payés" (II, iv). The second example

---

[22] See above, p. 51.

occurs in the other fight between Bougrelas and Ubu. Again it is Bougrelas who begins the volley of insults as he is beating Ubu in true *guignolesque* fashion: "Tiens, lâche, gueux, sacripant, mécréant, musulman" (V, ii). Ubu picks up the use of rhyme and riposts with an even longer and more fanciful list of insults as he in turn answers the blows of Bougrelas: "Tiens! Polognard, soûlard, bâtard, hussard, tartare, calard, cafard, mouchard, savoyard, communard" (V, ii). And Mère Ubu chimes in with yet another list of insults as she too joins the fight: "Tiens, capon, cochon, félon, histrion, fripon, souillon, polochon" (V, ii). It is obvious that the sound of the words plays the major role in these enumerations, and yet each epithet is by itself an appropriate or droll insult too. The constant repetition of sounds builds up to a verbal euphoria that underlines the farcical aspects of the action.

I have already mentioned several times the most important example of enumeration in *Ubu Roi,* which is the enumeration of tortures that comprise *le dernier supplice.* All of the elements of vocabulary and syntax employed here are cleverly woven together in this example of pure verbal virtuosity. It will be necessary to quote the entire text again in order to facilitate an analysis of it.

... torsion du nez, arrachement des cheveux, pénétration du petit bout de bois dans les oneilles, extraction de la cervelle par les talons, lacération du posterieur, suppression partielle ou même totale de la moelle épinière (si au moins ça pouvait lui ôter les épines du caractère), sans oublier l'ouverture de la vessie natatoire et finalement la grande décollation renouvelée de saint Jean-Baptiste, le tout tiré des très saintes Ecritures, tant de l'Ancien que du Nouveau Testament, mis en ordre, corrigé et perfectionné par l'ici présent Maître des Finances! Ça te va-t-il, andouille? (V, i)

First, let us notice that the use of noun phrases rather than verb phrases — especially since many of the nouns, such as *pénétration, extraction, lacération,* and *décollation* are Latinisms — is reminiscent of medieval penal terminology and gives a certain impression of pretentious abstraction to the list that is in contrast to the tortures themselves. Equally pretentious-sounding are the technical terms such as *la moelle épinière* and *la vessie natatoire.* The latter term is particularly comical because it refers to an organ that is found in fish rather than in human beings. Rhythm plays an important role also. From the relative simplicity of the first element there is an increase in complexity in each successive element which builds

up to "la mœlle épinière" at which point there is a break in the rhythm
by the abrupt inclusion of the pun on *épine*. This interruption provides
a brief pause before the final surge to "la grande décollation renouvelée
de saint Jean Baptiste," and the list terminates in a distorted burlesque
recitation of sacred texts of authority that would seem to permit or even
prescribe the tortures. The effect of this lengthy and complex tirade is
one of complete verbal intoxication; the words and phrases gather mo-
mentum until the language runs away with itself.

The only major example of pure jargon occurs in the last scene of the
play. This is the nautical language that is used during the flight by ship
of Ubu and *les Ubs* across the Baltic. This jargon probably affords us the
purest example of *fantaisie verbale* in the play. There are, in fact, two
categories of jargon found in this scene. First, there are the actual nautical
terms used by the captain of the boat, and, secondly, there are Ubu's
corruptions or distortions of these terms as he tries to assume control of
the vessel. Ubu's distortion of nautical terminology is accomplished in
several different manners: by the simple repetition of nautical terms in a
nonsensical or contradictory pattern or by making puns on them. Here
is a typical passage:

Le Commandant. N'arrivez pas, serrez près et plein!
Père Ubu. Si! Si! Arrivez. Je suis pressé, moi! Arrivez, entendez-vous! C'est
ta faute, brute de capitaine si nous n'arrivons pas. Nous devrions être arrivés.
Oh oh, mais je vais commander, moi, alors! Pare à virer! A Dieu vat!
Mouillez, virez vent devant, virez vent arrière. Hissez les voiles, serrez les
voiles, la barre dessus, la barre dessous, la barre à côté. Vous voyez, ça va
très bien. Venez en travers à la lame et alors ce sera parfait.
Le Commandant. Amenez le grand foc, prenez un ris aux humiers!
Père Ubu. Ceci n'est pas mal, c'est même bon! Entendez-vous, monsieur l'Equi-
page? Amenez le grand coq et allez faire un tour dans les pruniers. (V, iv)

As is frequently the case throughout the play, in addition to providing
some very comic dialogue, the language in this scene does contribute to
the characterization of Ubu. Most obviously, it demonstrates once again
his "bêtise." But on the other hand, it also shows the stubborn self-
assurance of his character that is such an essential element of a true
comic type. His good humor and his ability to make jokes are not at all
dampened by his defeat and by his being forced to flee the country. He
continues to make puns to the very last word of the play, which contains
a clever allusion to the original title, *Les Polonais,* which remains the

subtitle of *Ubu Roi*: "S'il n'y avait pas de Pologne, il n'y aurait pas de Polonais!" (V, iv).

The particular qualities of Ubu's language, which is, in fact, the dominant mode of the play, are emphasized by contrast with the more noble language used by some of the minor characters, notably King Venceslas, his family, and a few of the other "good" characters. Just as these characters are parodies of heroic types, so their language, especially that of Queen Rosemonde and Bougrelas, is mock-heroic. This fact is evident in the scene immediately preceding the assassination when Rosemonde is trying to persuade Venceslas not to attend the military review. For example, Venceslas heroically announces that not only will he go to the review, but will go unarmed: "Et vous, madame, pour vous prouver combien je crains peu M. Ubu, je vais aller à la revue comme je suis, sans arme et sans épée" (II, i). The Queen's reply is even more melodramatic: "Fatale imprudence, je ne vous reverrai pas vivant" (III, i).

The mock-heroic reaches its peak in the scene which follows the assassination. The situation is a parody of classic scenes of tragedy or melodrama. The Queen and the fourteen-year-old Prince have managed to escape miraculously from the clutches of the wicked usurper. They have just reached a cavern in the mountains where they hope to be safe, but the Queen is rapidly failing after so many tragedies, and she announces sadly that she is going to die: "Je n'en ai plus que deux heures à vivre" (II, v). When Bougrelas expresses some surprise, she explains:

Comment veux-tu que je résiste à tant de coups? Le roi massacré, notre famille détruite, et toi, représentant de la plus noble race qui ait jamais porté l'épée, forcé de t'enfuir dans les montagnes comme un contrebandier. (II, v)

Bougrelas tries courageously to cheer his mother: "Attendons avec espérance et ne renonçons jamais à nos droits" (II, v). But the Queen melodramatically replies: "Je te le souhaite, mon cher enfant, mais pour moi, je ne verrai pas cet heureux jour" (II, v). And with these words, she dies. It is now Bougrelas' turn to be melodramatic:

Eh! qu'as tu? Elle pâlit, elle tombe. Au secours! Mais je suis dans un désert! O mon Dieu! Son cœur ne bat plus. Elle est morte. Est-ce possible? Encore une victime du Père Ubu! O mon Dieu! qu'il est triste de se voir à quatorze ans avec une vengeance terrible à poursuivre! (II, v)

While he is overcome with despair, the ghosts of his dead family and all his ancestors enter the cave, and, in a scene that is an obvious parody of *Hamlet*, one of them gives him a sword and announces that he must avenge their name: "Et que cette épée que je te donne n'ait de repos que quand elle aura frappé de mort l'usurpateur" (II, v).

There are several scenes in which all the elements of situation, action, characterization, and style are skillfully woven together to form a harmonious and extremely comic unit. I have already analyzed these scenes from the points of view of situation, action, and characterization. It is also necessary to make an analysis of all the various aspects of style used in these scenes.

The first of these is the scene or episode of the battle with the Russians. It is at the beginning of this episode that Ubu comes on stage dragging his horse behind him and makes the comically pompous speech about his fatigue. A moment later, Nicholas Rensky enters with the news that Bougrelas and his partisans have chased Mère Ubu out of the capital. Ubu's response is quite colorful with its unusual images, especially the *hibou à guêtres*, its repetition, and its colloquialism: "Oiseau de nuit, bête de malheur, hibou à guêtres! Où as-tu pêché ces sornettes? En voilà d'une autre! Et qui a fait ça? Bougrelas, je parie. D'où viens-tu?" (IV, iii). Rensky answers that he has come from Warsaw, and Ubu continues in the same vein:

Garçon de ma merdre, si je t'en croyais je ferais rebrousser chemin à toute l'armée. Mais, Seigneur garçon, il y a sur tes épaules plus de plumes que de cervelle et tu as rêvé des sottises. Va aux avant-postes, mon garçon, les Russes ne sont pas loin et nous aurons bientôt à estocader de nos armes, tant à merdre qu'à phynances et à physique. (IV, iii)

Just at that moment, the Russians are sighted on the plain below the hill on which they are situated. There is no way to escape, and Ubu is forced to make plans for battle. His speech is an eloquent burlesque of military strategy:

Allons, messieurs, prenons nos dispositions pour la bataille. Nous allons rester sur la colline et ne commettrons point la sottise de descendre en bas. Je me tiendrai au milieu comme une citadelle vivante et vous autres graviterez autour de moi. J'ai à vous recommander de mettre dans les fusils autant de balles qu'ils en pourront tenir, car 8 balles peuvent tuer 8 Russes et c'est autant que je n'aurai pas sur le dos. Nous mettrons les fantassins à pied au bas de la colline pour recevoir les Russes et les tuer un peu, les cavaliers derrière pour se jeter dans la confusion, et l'artillerie autour du moulin à vent ici présent pour tirer dans le tas. Quant à nous, nous nous tiendrons dans le moulin à vent et tirerons avec le pistolet à phynances par la fenêtre, en travers de la porte nous placerons le bâton à physique, et si quelqu'un essaye d'entrer gare au croc à merdre!!! (IV, iii)

The dialogue during the battle sequence is as broadly farcical as is the action. Several of the speeches which have already been quoted as examples of the various comic techniques come from this episode, for instance Ubu's complaints and his exhortation to his weapons. Ubu uses numerous colloquial or trite expressions during the battle which are particularly inappropriate to the seriousness of a real battle and therefore seem especially comic. They also underline Ubu's complete unfitness for the role of warrior king. When a captain announces that the Russians are attacking, Ubu's reaction is more befitting that of a street cleaner than a king: "Eh bien! après, que veux-tu que j'y fasse? Ce n'est pas moi qui le leur ai dit." It also reveals his basic cowardice.

Ubu uses similar language when he attacks the Czar and, in a quick reversal, is himself put to flight. We can actually visualize the action through the dialogue here. "Tiens, toi! oh! aïe! Ah! mais tout de même. Ah! monsieur, pardon, laissez-moi tranquille. Oh! mais, je n'ai pas fait exprès!" (IV, iv). It is at this point that we have the pantomime of the chase on horseback during which the Czar falls in a ditch. As soon as Ubu realizes that he is no longer being pursued, he launches into a tirade that is a model of *fantaisie verbale*:

Ah! j'ose à peine me retourner! Il est dedans. Ah! c'est bien fait et on tape dessus. Allons, Polonais, allez-y à tour de bras, il a bon dos, le misérable! Moi, je n'ose pas le regarder! Et cependant, notre prédiction s'est complètement réalisé, le bâton à physique a fait merveilles et nul doute que je ne l'eusse complètement tué si une inexplicable terreur n'était venue combattre et annuler en nous les effets de notre courage. Mais nous avons dû soudainement tourner casaque, et nous n'avons dû notre salut qu'à notre habilité comme cavalier ainsi qu'à la solidité des jarrets de notre cheval à finances, dont la rapidité n'a d'égale que la solidité et dont la légèreté fait la célébrité, ainsi qu'à la profondeur du fossé qui s'est trouvé fort à propos sous les pas de l'ennemi de nous l'ici présent Maître des Phynances. Tout ceci est fort beau, mais personne ne m'écoute. Allons! bon, ça recommence! (IV, iv)

Another episode in which the style is perfectly suited to, and enhances, the comedy of character and action is the episode of the fight with the bear. The episode begins on an unusually ridiculous note. When the bear first enters the cave, Ubu mistakes it for a dog and refers to it with a hypocorism: "Oh! tiens, regardez donc le petit toutou. Il est gentil, ma foi" (IV, vi). As soon as he realizes it is a bear, his tone changes abruptly into a characteristically exaggerated and comical expression of fear: "Un ours! Ah! l'atroce bête. Oh! pauvre homme, me voilà mangé. Que Dieu me protège! Et il vient sur moi. Non, c'est Cotice qu'il attrape. Ah! je respire" (IV, vi). Ubu then climbs up on a rock and begins saying the Pater Noster while Pile and Cotice struggle with the bear. The dialogue in this episode further demonstrates Ubu's cowardice, his total lack of concern for others, and his self-satisfied braggadocio. The chanting of the Pater Noster in Latin also provides an ironic counterpoint to and commentary on the violent and farcical action that is taking place on stage. For example, when Pile says "Ah! il me mord! O Seigneur, sauvez-nous, je suis mort" (IV, vi), Ubu piously chants "Fiat voluntas tua!" (IV, vi). And when Cotice finally succeeds in shooting the bear, Ubu appropriately intones: "Sed libera nos à malo. Amen" (IV, vi). The use of Latin also provides another example of jargon which is an element of *fantaisie verbale*. But the real masterpiece of *fantaisie verbale* in this scene is the speech which Ubu delivers while he is descending from the rock. Ubu's relief and sense of well-being from having escaped the danger presented by the bear are translated into a joyful intoxication of language.

Vous pouvez vous flatter que si vous êtes encore vivants et si vous foulez encore la neige de Lithuanie, vous le devez à la vertu magnanime du Maître des Finances, qui s'est évertué, échiné, et égosillé à débiter des patenôtres pour votre salut, et qui a manié avec autant de courage le glaive spirituel de la prière que vous avez manié avec adresse le temporel de l'ici présent Palotin Cotice coup-de-poing explosif. Nous avons même poussé plus loin notre dévouement, car nous n'avons pas hésité à monter sur un rocher plus fort pour que nos prières aient moins loin à arriver au ciel. (IV, vi)

Pile, who was half-devoured by the bear, comments in utter disgust: "Révoltante bourrique!" (IV, vi). Ubu is completely undaunted, however, and he continues by making a pretentiously ingenious pun on the size of the bear:

Voici une grosse bête. Grace à moi, vous avez de quoi souper. Quel ventre, messieurs! Les Grecs y auraient été plus à l'aise que dans le cheval de bois, et peu s'en est fallu, chers amis, que nous n'ayons pu aller vérifier de nos propres yeux sa capacité intérieure. (IV, vi)

Later in the scene when Pile remarks that the bear is already cold, Ubu makes another grotesque witticism: "C'est dommage, il aurait mieux valu le manger chaud. Ceci va procurer une indigestion au Maître des Finances" (IV, vi). It is also in this scene that Ubu makes a statement of pure nonsense that is worthy of Joseph Prud'homme: "Je vais allumer du feu en attendant qu'il apporte du bois" (IV, vi).

The climax of the play from the point of view of style or comic dialogue comes in the apparition scene in Act V. All of the stylistic techniques and devices already described — pun, play on words, nonsense, parody, jargon, platitudes, repetition, and accumulation — are used in this scene in which Père and Mère Ubu fight a uniquely comical duel with insults. The scene opens with Mère Ubu's soliloquy in which she recounts how she was chased from the capital and pursued for four days by Bougrelas and his partisans before finding refuge in the very same cave that, unbeknown to her, is harboring her husband. Her long speech is in itself a masterful parody of such traditional soliloquies in its clever mixture of contrasting language and tone. I have already quoted part of her droll statement about the Palotin Giron's attachment to her. [23] She continues in the same vein: "Il se serait fait couper en deux pour moi, le pauvre garçon. La preuve, c'est qu'il a été coupé en quatre par Bougrelas. Pif paf pan!" (V, i). Then she switches back to a recital of the events of her escape in mock-heroic language. Here is a sample:

De tous côtés la noblesse se rassemble et me poursuit. Je manque mille fois périr, étouffée dans un cercle de Polonais acharnés à me perdre. Enfin je trompai leur fureur, et après quatre jours de courses dans la neige de ce qui fut mon royaume, j'arrive me réfugier ici. (V, i)

Her thoughts then turn to her husband and there is a sudden reversal in her language to a more colloquial tone:

Mais je voudrais bien savoir ce qu'est devenu mon gros polichinelle, je veux dire mon très respectable époux. Lui en ai-je pris de la finance! Lui en ai-je volé, des rixdales! Lui en ai-je tiré, des carottes! Et son cheval à finances qui mourrait de faim: il ne voyait pas souvent d'avoine, le pauvre diable. Ah! la bonne histoire. (V, i)

---

[23] See above, p. 64.

This episode leads directly into Mère Ubu's discovery that her *gros polichinelle* is there in the cave with her. Then begins the verbal sword-play between them.

Mère Ubu begins by affecting language with a biblical flavor in order to persuade Ubu that she is Saint Gabriel.

Oui, monsieur Ubu, on parle, en effet, et la trompette de l'archange qui doit tirer les morts de la cendre et de la poussière finale ne parlerait pas autrement! Ecoutez cette voix sévère. C'est celle de saint Gabriel qui ne peut donner que de bons conseils. (V, i)

Ubu is not at all impressed, however, and responds with a familiar expression: "Oh! ça, en effet!" (V, i). But then Mère Ubu threatens him in language that he understands: "Ne m'interrompez pas ou je me tais et c'en sera fait de votre giborgne!" (V, i). This time, he replies more politely: "Je me tais, je ne dis plus mot. Continuez, Mme l'Apparition" (V, i). But of course his impertinence returns at once, and when Mère Ubu calls him *un gros bonhomme,* he replies with a pun: "Très gros, en effet, ceci est juste" (V, i). Puns, plays on words, repetitions, and antitheses continue throughout the scene as Ubu parries each thrust of Mère Ubu.

The lengthy scene can be divided into several groups of interchanges. The first group is built around Mère Ubu's efforts to convince Père Ubu that his wife, that is she herself, is faultless. But naturally Ubu counters each flattering remark she makes with an insult. Here is an example of dialogue which contains some of the devices mentioned:

Mère Ubu. ... Vous êtes marié, monsieur Ubu?
Père Ubu. Parfaitement, à la dernière des chipies!
Mère Ubu. Vous voulez dire que c'est une femme charmante.
Père Ubu. Une horreur. Elle a des griffes partout, on ne sait par où la prendre.
Mère Ubu. Il faut la prendre par la douceur, sire Ubu, et si vous la prenez ainsi vous verrez qu'elle est au moins l'égale de la Vénus de Capoue.
Père Ubu. Qui dites-vous qui a des poux? (V, i)

This section ends with particularly skillful repartee:

Mère Ubu. Tout ceci sont des mensonges, votre femme est un modèle, et vous, quel monstre vous faites.
Père Ubu. Tout ceci sont des vérités. Ma femme est une coquine et vous, quelle andouille vous faites. (V, i)

Having lost this round, Mère Ubu changes tactics and begins to attack Ubu with accusations of his numerous crimes. She makes a major error, however, in forgetting that Ubu has no sense of remorse. He parries these thrusts just as easily as he did the others. For example, when she accuses him of mistreating Bordure, he replies: "J'aime mieux que ce soit moi que lui qui règne en Lithuanie. Pour le moment, ça n'est ni l'un ni l'autre. Ainsi, vous voyez que ce n'est pas moi" (V, i).

But her worst mistake is in revealing to Ubu that she was stealing money from him. He expresses his satisfaction at learning this news in a burst of verbal virtuosity that approaches *la fantaisie verbale*:

Mais enfin je suis content de savoir maintenant assurément que ma chère épouse me volait. Je le sais maintenant de source sure. Omnis a Déo scientia, ce qui veut dire: omnis, toute; a Déo, science; scientia, vient de Dieu. Voilà l'explication du phénomène. Mais Madame l'Apparition ne dit plus rien! Que ne puis-je lui offrir de quoi se réconforter! Ce qu'elle disait était très amusant.... (V, i)

The sun rises at this opportune moment, Ubu discovers Mère Ubu, and the duel continues with renewed vigor.

Père Ubu. . . . Tiens, mais il fait jour. Ah! Seigneur, de par mon cheval à finances, c'est la Mère Ubu!

Mère Ubu, effrontément. Ça n'est pas vrai, je vais vous excommunier.

Père Ubu. Ah! charogne!

Mère Ubu. Quelle impiété!

Père Ubu. Ah! c'est trop fort. Je vois bien que c'est toi, sotte chipie! Pourquoi diable es-tu ici?

Mère Ubu. Giron est mort et les Polonais m'ont chassée.

Père Ubu. Et moi, ce sont les Russes qui m'ont chassé: les beaux esprits se rencontrent.

Mère Ubu. Dis donc qu'un bel esprit a rencontré une bourrique!

Père Ubu. Ah! eh bien, il va rencontrer un palmipède maintenant. (Il lui jette l'ours.) (V, i)

Mère Ubu's complaints as she struggles under the weight of the dead bear are as exaggerated and colorful as those of her husband. "Ah! grand Dieu! Quelle horreur! Ah! je meurs! j'étouffe! il me mord! il m'avale! il me digère!" (V, i). She is so convincing that Ubu thinks that the bear is not dead, climbs back onto his rock, and begins chanting the Pater Noster. When Mère Ubu finally extricates herself from the bear skin and asks Ubu how the dead bear got there, he confusedly replies: "Je ne sais pas. Ah! si, je sais! Il a voulu manger Pile et Cotice et moi je l'ai tué d'un coup de Pater Noster" (V, i). This line is quite amusing in that the audience is aware of the allusion Ubu is making to an episode that was in itself particularly farcical although it appears to be utter nonsense to Mère Ubu. Her response is predictable, as is Ubu's next reply:

Mère Ubu.   Qu'est-ce que c'est que ça? Il est fou, ma finance!
Père Ubu.   C'est très exact ce que je dis! Et toi, tu es idiote, ma giborgne!
   (V, i)

They finally begin to recount their experiences to each other in a final group of interchanges that pivots on the repetition of the sentence: "Ça m'est bien égal."

Père Ubu.   J'ai cru qu'on voulait m'écarteler. Oh! les enragés! Et puis ils ont tué Rensky!
Mère Ubu.   Ça m'est bien égal! Tu sais que Bougrelas a tué le Palotin Giron!
Père Ubu.   Ça m'est bien égal! Et puis, ils ont tué le pauvre Lascy!
Mère Ubu.   Ça m'est bien égal! (V, i)

The rhythm of the dialogue in this last group of interchanges has increased to a peak of intensity. Ubu then seizes Mère Ubu, throws her to her knees, and delivers the long and elaborate threat of *le dernier supplice,* already quoted in full, which ends the scene with a crashing finale.

The dialogue of this scene provides a perfect example of all the elements of vocabulary and rhetorical devices and techniques that make up the style of *Ubu Roi.* It also demonstrates how the style both reflects and contributes to the other elements of the play, that is the plot, the action, and, especially, the characterization. And finally, this scene shows how the style or dialogue makes an essential contribution to the comedy of the play.

It has often been observed that the tendency to enjoy playing with the sound of words is characteristic of children. Ubu's playful use of language, then, reflects his childish or elemental mentality. Again, one can trace some aspects of the style of *Ubu* back to the origins of the play at the Lycée de Rennes. Robert Garapon, in his study of "la fantaisie verbale" in the theater, makes a direct association between the youthful delight in playing with language and the prevalence of wordplay in the *sotties,* farces, and comedies of the Middle Ages, a period which represented, in a sense, the childhood of the French language and the French theater. *Ubu Roi,* in many ways, marks a return to the most basic elements and forms of comedy.

The style of the play also takes on symbolic significance and functions as part of the satire. "Le parler Ubu" is only a slightly distorted version of our own language and that of our most sacred institutions. As with Ubu, our pompous verbosity frequently breaks down or runs away with itself like a machine gone mad. But language is not only a mirror of a society; on a more general level, it is an outward manifestation of man's basic nature. The language of *Ubu Roi* reflects Jarry's view of the human soul as grotesque and absurd. The first word of the play does indeed set the tone for all that is to follow. The audience at the first performance reacted to that initial *merdre* as if it were a battle cry. In a sense, it was.

CONCLUSION

It is a curious but not insignificant fact that it all began with a simple schoolboy joke, a satire of a hated professor and an adolescent mockery of established forms of authority. The adolescent mentality that first created Ubu is reflected in both the subject matter and the form of the play. It reveals itself in the obscenity, in the gratuitous ferocity, in the slapstick, in the stereotyped characters, in the elementary parody, and in the verbal play. But this same primitivism of subject matter and style is part of Ubu's unique and important contribution to the modern theater. The elemental aspects of Ubu's nature are precisely those which give universal validity to his character. Ubu — puppet, clown, buffoon — is a reflection, albeit distorted, of the inner nature of mankind. Or, to use Freudian terminology, he is the universal Id.

Jarry himself was not aware of the full import of Ubu until he went to Paris and became associated with the Parisian artistic and literary milieu out of which have come so many of the experimental and revolutionary techniques and movements of this century. One of his most important contacts was with the master of symbolism, Stéphane Mallarmé, who had already made several pleas for a revolt against the traditionally rational theater of the day and had called for a theater of irrationality, of myth and fable, "vierge de tout, lieu, temps et personne sus. . . . " [1]

The influence of symbolism is quite apparent in the poetry and prose that Jarry wrote during the years 1894 to 1896 which include *Les Minutes de Sable Mémorial* and *César-Antéchrist*. It is also quite significant that these two works incorporated parts of the Ubu cycle that

---

[1] "Richard Wagner, Rêverie d'un poète français," *Œuvres complètes* (Paris: Bibliothèque de la Pléiade, 1945), p. 544.

Jarry had brought to Paris with him. It indicates that Jarry was becoming increasingly aware of the symbolic suggestiveness of the figure of Ubu. Unlike the Morin brothers, who later dismissed their part in the schoolboy satire as having been a childish prank, Jarry realized that their overgrown puppet could represent "tout le grotesque . . . au monde" to a mature audience as well as to a group of schoolboys.

Jarry's theories of dramatic technique developed naturally from his experiences in staging *Ubu Roi*. They first found expression in the letter Jarry wrote to Lugné-Poe in January, 1896, in which he discussed the possibility of producing the play at the Théâtre de l'Œuvre. I have already had occasion to mention some of Jarry's suggestions as to the manner of staging the play. They all pointed to the kind of stylization that is typical of the marionette theater: the use of a mask for the main character, the adoption of a special accent or voice by the actor who played this role, and the use of cardboard horses' heads in the equestrian scenes. The two paragraphs dealing with scenery and costumes contained suggestions that were particularly representative of the line of development of Jarry's ideas:

3. Adoption d'un seul décor, ou mieux, d'un fond uni supprimant les levers et baissers de rideau pendant l'acte unique. Un personnage correctement vêtu viendrait, comme dans les guignols, accrocher une pancarte signifiant le lieu de la scène. (Notez que je suis certain de la supériorité "suggestive" de la pancarte écrite sur le décor. Un décor, ni une figuration, ne rendraient "l'armée polonaise en marche dans l'Ukraine.")

... ...

6. Costumes aussi peu couleur locale ou chronologiques que possible (ce qui rend mieux l'idée d'une chose éternelle), moderne de préférence, puisque la satire est moderne; et sordide, parce que le drame en paraît plus misérable et horrifique. [2]

That Jarry was becoming conscious of his role as an innovator was clearly revealed in later letters to Lugné-Poe about the forthcoming production of the play. Another revolutionary idea that he proposed was to use a young boy for the role of Bougrelas, a role that would be played by a woman according to the traditions of the day. In the letter in which he mentioned this idea, Jarry was quite obviously rebelling against this and other theatrical traditions that he considered to be sterile.

---

[2] In *Tout Ubu*, p. 124.

Ne pensez-vous pas qu'il serait peut-être amusant, pour que tout soit nouveau quand on montera *Ubu,* de faire jouer Bougrelas par un gosse intelligent de l'âge requis et de réagir ainsi contre une tradition de travesti que personne n'a osé démolir depuis une phrase de la préface du *Mariage de Figaro?* [3]

The ideas that Jarry had first expressed to Lugné-Poe in January, 1896, reappeared in the two brief articles which he wrote for the production of the play at the end of that same year, i.e. the Preliminary Address that Jarry read and the brochure that was distributed to the audience. [4] In the Preliminary Address Jarry stressed again the *guignolesque* aspects of the play, and in the brochure he emphasized the universality of the character of Ubu.

Another article dealing specifically with the Ubu plays, "Les Paralipomènes d'Ubu," was published in *La Revue Blanche* a few days before the performance of *Ubu Roi.* In this article, Jarry also discussed the character of Ubu, mentioned the entire legend and cycle of plays, and included several scenes from *Ubu Cocu.*

Jarry's ideas on theatrical technique were more generalized in the article "De l'inutilité du théâtre au théâtre" which appeared in *Le Mercure de France* in September, 1896. However, Jarry did comment in one of his letters to Lugné-Poe: "Mon article du *Mercure* ... n'est pas une théorie complète parce que j'ai pensé surtout à la mise en scène d'Ubu." [5] Again Jarry reworked and developed some of the ideas he had already expressed in his first letter to Lugné-Poe, among them his theories about scenery and masks. His rebellion against sterile traditions and his growing scorn for a public who insisted on these same traditions were particularly evident in this article. His discussion of trompe-l'œil scenery was a frontal assault on the use of scenery to create an illusion of reality which was a prevailing trend in both the *théâtre du boulevard* and in the realistic and naturalistic drama.

Il y a deux sortes de décors, intérieurs et sous le ciel. Toutes deux ont la prétention de représenter des salles ou des champs naturels. Nous ne reviendrons pas sur la question entendue une fois pour toutes de la stupidité du trompe-l'œil. Mentionnons que ledit trompe-l'œil fait allusion à celui qui voit grossièrement,

---

[3] *Ibid.,* p. 125.
[4] *Ibid.,* pp. 19-20, 21-22.
[5] *Iibd.,* p. 127.

c'est-a-dire ne voit pas, et scandalise qui voit d'une façon intelligente et éligente la nature, lui en présentant la caricature par celui qui ne comprend pas. [6]

Jarry's ideas of acting techniques and character portrayal were also anti-realistic. He expanded upon his idea of using masks which, he said, should represent the essence of the character:

L'acteur devra substituer à sa tête, au moyen d'un *masque* l'enfermant, l'effigie du PERSONNAGE, laquelle n'aura pas, comme à l'antique, caractère de pleurs ou de rire (ce qui n'est pas un caractère), mais caractère du personnage: l'Avare, l'Hésitant, l'Avide entassant les crimes. . . . [7]

Varieties of facial expression could be achieved, according to Jarry, by the skillful use of lighting in conjunction with movement by the actor:

Par de lents hochements de haut en bas et bas en haut et librations latérales, l'acteur déplace les ombres sur toute la surface de son masque. Et l'expérience prouve que les six positions principales . . . suffisent à toutes les expressions. [8]

His theory of acting technique thus approaches the techniques of pantomime, but he condemns the sterile conventions of pantomime as categorically as those of the realistic and naturalistic schools. What Jarry repeatedly called for was the gesture that through its simplicity and universality would express the very essence of humanity embodied within the character type.

Jarry's attack on the theater public was even more intense in the article "Questions de théâtre" which was published in *La Revue Blanche* in response to the storm of criticism that followed the first performance of *Ubu Roi*. Jarry presented several important ideas in this article both in relation to *Ubu* and to the theater in general. First he defined the main purpose of a play as being the revelation of a character. If the action revolved around one central character, it would render unnecessary the strict observance of the traditional dramatic unities of time, place, and action.

Secondly, Jarry further emphasized the satirical aspect of the character of Ubu which he had mentioned briefly and in much more general terms

---

[6] *Ibid.,* p. 130.
[7] *Ibid.,* p. 131.
[8] *Ibid.,* p. 132.

in preceding articles. This time, he bluntly stated that Ubu was indeed a direct attack on the theater audience through the presentation, only slightly distorted, of its "double ignoble." In several random remarks Jarry also included bits of literary criticism. He revealed his total contempt for the dramatists whose works were very popular in his day, Augier, Dumas fils, Labiche, and others. And he declared his admiration for other writers and works associated directly or indirectly with the Symbolist Movement and its basic techniques such as Baudelaire, Rimbaud, Verlaine, Mallarmé, and the plays *Peer Gynt, Les Flaireurs,* and *Pelléas et Mélisande.*

Several fragments containing brief observations on the theater were published posthumously in the *Dossiers acénonètes du Collège de 'Pataphysique* [9] and later included in *Tout Ubu* under the title "Douze arguments sur le théâtre." In these fragments, Jarry continued to develop his concept of the conflict between the artist and the general public. He condemned categorically the works of art that appealed to the crowd and praised highly those that were directed to the elite audience that frequented the small avant-garde theaters such as the Théâtre d'Art and the Théâtre de l'Œuvre. He spoke with increasing confidence of a rebirth in the theater that he saw taking place in these and other small "théâtres à côtés." He called this new theater, and the capitals are his, "un théâtre ABSTRAIT."

One of the most interesting and significant ideas presented in this article was that dramatic literature is a genre unto itself the nature of which is distinct from that of any other literary genre and which must necessarily follow different rules of construction from its very inception. A novel adapted for the stage did not constitute a true example of dramatic literature, according to Jarry. Again, he stated that one of the main purposes of a dramatic work was to present a new human type. He even went so far as to say: "Si l'on ne peut absolument créer, c'est-à-dire faire naître un être nouveau, qu'on se tienne tranquille." [10]

These articles constitute the major part of Jarry's theatrical manifesto. In them we can see him moving from specific ideas about the staging of *Ubu Roi* to a new and revolutionary theory of total theater. The new theater that he advocated, which he called an abstract theater, was a

---

[9] No. 5 [1959], 1-6.
[10] *Tout Ubu,* p. 136.

synthesis of techniques and principles of the marionette theater, of the formal traditions of pantomime, and of the Symbolist Movement in literature. What Jarry had come to realize was that the "slice of life" realism or the comedy of manners reflected only the superficial realities of life and that the deeper realities of human existence could best be revealed through the use of symbols or signs. He also was aware that all of the techniques for staging a play — scenery, lighting, costumes, and acting — can take on symbolic significance as well as that which is incorporated into the text of the play itself. The theories that Jarry expressed, in conjunction with the example that he gave with *Ubu Roi*, have had a profound influence upon the entire modern theater as well as on other forms of literature and art.

Many of the themes and techniques that were present in *Ubu* or that Jarry discussed in his writings on the theater have become important motifs in modern art and literature and especially in the contemporary avant-garde drama. The figure of the puppet or clown has become an equation for the human condition in the modern world. It is an image that contains multiple allusions, all of which are equally meaningful. It can be an image of man's helplessness to control his own destiny either because of tendencies within himself or of factors outside himself over which he has no control. Indeed the mechanical goose-stepping of the Nazi soldiers has given contemporary emphasis to this aspect of the puppet as symbol. Or, as in Samuel Beckett's play, *En attendant Godot,* the clown or buffoon can present an image of perplexity, a being who is faced with the absurdity or meaninglessness of life. Another important aspect of the figure of the puppet or clown is that it has traditionally incorporated elements of both the tragic and the comic. If tragedy is in fact dead, as George Steiner has suggested, [11] then what more fitting replacement for the tragic hero can we find than the puppet or clown? From yet another point of view, if we follow Henri Bergson's theory of the comic as something mechanical encrusted on the living [12] to its logical conclusion, then we see that the puppet figure embodies the very essence of comedy.

---

[11] See *The Death of Tragedy* (New York: Alfred Knopf, 1961).

[12] See Henri Bergson, *Le Rire. Essai sur la signification du comique,* in *Œuvres* (Paris: Presses Universitaires de France, 1959).

Another motif which has gained increasing significance in modern art and literature and which is related to the puppet in some respects is the motif of the mask. Again it is a device that contains multiple allusions. Following the example of *Ubu Roi* and the suggestions of Jarry, the mask has often been used by a kind of inverse logic as a physical means of reflecting the inner reality of a character through the exaggeration or crystalization of a single character trait. An interesting example of the use of this aspect of the motif of the mask can be found in the title of the collected edition of the plays of Luigi Pirandello, *Maschere nude* or "Naked Masks." Or the mask can be used as the symbol of the role or roles the individual plays or is forced to play in society. In a play like Jean Genet's *Les Nègres,* the actors can change roles during the course of the play by assuming, removing, or exchanging masks.

Violence in all its many forms has undoubtedly become a central theme in modern literature and drama. Ubu's gratuitous ferocity has been so overshadowed by actual events of history that it no longer seems exaggerated or shocking. His unblushing enjoyment of his own ferocity remains perhaps his only singularity. Similarly, Ubu's obscenity that shocked and stunned theater audiences in 1896 has long since been outdone by works aimed at a much larger audience. But we must still give the credit to Jarry for having been the first to burst the dam of literary and theatrical propriety.

It is not just isolated themes and techniques of *Ubu Roi* that have had an influence on the modern theater. The general atmosphere or mode of *Ubu* has become the dominant mode of an entire group of contemporary plays that have been given the appellation of the Theater of the Absurd. There are several characteristics which are basic to this type of play and which these plays have in common with *Ubu Roi.* There is a total disregard for, if not deliberate flaunting of, conventional realism, which often creates a dream-like or hallucinatory atmosphere and one that tends frequently to be nightmarish. A similar lack of orthodoxy and realism is present in the language or dialogue which includes verbal fantasy, nonsense, and sometimes a total breakdown of meaning. But the most important characteristic of these plays and the one which more than the others makes them deserving of their appellation is a new and peculiar mixture of tragic and comic elements. Broad clowning and ribald farce accompany or alternate with actions or scenes of violence and horror. The general atmosphere or mood that is created, then, can be characterized as being grotesque or absurd.

Martin Esslin, in his study on *The Theater of the Absurd,* argues quite convincingly that this new type of play is the one best suited to express the realities of life in the twentieth century with its own distinctive attitudes, preoccupations, and anxieties. He states:

... The Theater of the Absurd ... can be seen as the reflection of what seems the attitude most genuinely representative of our own time's contribution.

The hallmark of this attitude is its sense that the certitudes and unshakable basic assumptions of former ages have been tested and found wanting, that they have been discredited as cheap and somewhat childish illusions. [13]

Eugene Ionesco, one of the major playwrights of the Theater of the Absurd, gives this definition of the term absurd:

Est absurde ce qui n'a pas de but ... Coupé de ses racines religieuses ou métaphysiques ou transcendantales, l'homme est perdu, toute sa démarche devient insensée, absurde, inutile, étouffante. [14]

Ubu's exclamation was indeed prophetic: "Ah! saleté! le mauvais droit ne vaut-il pas le bon?" (III, i).

According to Mr. Esslin, what makes this new kind of play particularly apt as an artistic expression of the absurdity of the human condition is that it presents this absurdity in the form of the plays as well as in the subject matter. As Mr. Esslin states,

The Theater of the Absurd has renounced arguing *about* the absurdity of the human condition; it merely *presents* it in being — that is, in terms of concrete stage images of the absurdity of existence. [15]

William Butler Yeats' sorrowful prediction, made after having attended the first performance of *Ubu Roi,* has indeed come true; the "Savage God" is here to stay.

---

[13] P. xviii.

[14] "Dans les Armes de la Ville," *Cahiers de la Compagnie Madeleine Renaud - Jean-Louis Barrault,* 20 (October, 1957), 4.

[15] Esslin, *op. cit.,* p. xx.

BIBLIOGRAPHY

I. GENERAL BIBLIOGRAPHY

Artaud, Antonin. *Le Théâtre et son double*. Paris: Gallimard, 1938.

Bergson, Henri. *Le Rire. Essai sur la signification du comique*. In *Œuvres*. Paris: Presses Universitaires de France, 1959.

Brustein, Robert. *The Theater of Revolt*. Boston: Atlantic—Little, Brown and Co., n. d.

Calvet, J. *Les Types universels dans la littérature française*. Paris: F. Lanore, 1932.

Celler, Ludovic. *Les Types populaires au théâtre*. Paris: Liepmannsohn et Dufour, 1870.

Cohn, Ruby. *Currents in Contemporary Drama*. Bloomington and London: Indiana University Press, 1969.

Coindreau, Maurice Edgar. *La Farce est jouée. Vingt-cinq ans de théâtre français*. New York: Editions de la Maison Française, 1942.

Cook, Albert. *The Dark Voyage and the Golden Mean*. Cambridge: Harvard University Press, 1949.

Dumur, Louis. "Variétés: Polti, 'Les Tendances actuelles du théâtre en France.' " *Mercure de France*, 16 (January, 1902), 280-284.

Esslin, Martin. *The Theater of the Absurd*. Anchor Books. Garden City, New York: Doubleday and Co., Inc., 1961.

Feibleman, James. *In Praise of Comedy*. New York: The Macmillan Co., 1939.

Fort, Paul. *Mes Mémoires: Toute la vie d'un poète*. Paris: Flammarion, 1944.

Fowlie, Wallace. *Dionysus in Paris. A Guide to Contemporary French Theater*. New York: Meridian Books, Inc., 1960.

Garapon, Robert. *La Fantaisie verbale et le comique dans le théâtre du moyen âge jusqu'à la fin du XVIIᵉ siècle*. Paris: Librairie Armand Colin, 1957.

Gouhier, Henri. *L'Œuvre théâtrale*. Bibliothèque d'Esthétique. Paris: Flammarion, 1958.

Guichardnaud, Jacques. *The Modern French Theater*. New Haven: Yale University Press, 1961.

Ionesco, Eugène. "Dans les armes de la ville." *Cahiers de la Compagnie Madeleine Renaud - Jean-Louis Barrault*, 20 (October, 1957), 3-5.

Jasper, Gertrude Rathbone. *Adventures in the Theater: Lugné-Poe and the Théâtre de l'Œuvre to 1899*. New Brunswick, New Jersey: Rutgers University Press, 1947.

Knapp, Bettina L. *Antonin Artaud: Man of Vision.* New York: David Lewis, 1969.

Langer, Suzanne K. *Feeling and Form.* New York: Charles Scribner's Sons, 1953.

Lauter, Paul. *Theories of Comedy.* Anchor Books. Garden City, New York: Doubleday and Co., 1964.

Lugné-Poe, A. F. *La Parade: Acrobaties.* 3ʳᵈ ed. Paris: Gallimard, 1931.

――――. *La Parade: Dernière pirouette.* Paris: Sagittaire, 1946.

Mallarmé, Stéphane. *Propos sur la poésie.* Ed. H. Mondor. Monaco: Editions du Rocher, 1953.

Pronko, Leonard Cabell. *Avant-Garde: The Experimental Theater in France.* Berkeley and Los Angeles: University of California Press, 1962.

Raymond, Marcel. *De Baudelaire au Surréalisme. Essai sur le mouvement poétique contemporain.* Paris: Editions R.-A. Corréa, 1933.

Robichez, Jacques. *Le Symbolisme au théâtre.* Paris: L'Arche, 1957.

Serreau, Geneviève. *L'Histoire du "nouveau théâtre."* Collection Idées. Paris: Gallimard, 1966.

Styan, J. L. *The Dark Comedy. The Development of Modern Comic Tragedy.* Cambridge, England: Cambridge University Press, 1962.

Symons, Arthur. *Studies in Seven Arts.* New York: E. P. Dutton and Co., 1907.

Sypher, Wylie, ed. *Comedy.* Anchor Books. Garden City, New York: Doubleday and Co., 1956.

Wellwarth, George. *The Theater of Protest and Paradox, Developments in the Avant-Garde Drama.* New York: New York University Press, 1964.

Worcester, David. *The Art of Satire.* Cambridge: Harvard University Press, 1940.

Yale French Studies, 23 (Summer, 1959). Issue on "Humor."

II. WORKS ON JARRY AND *Ubu Roi*

A. BIBLIOGRAPHIES

Cahiers du Collège de 'Pataphysique, 10 [1953]. "L'Expojarrysition." Contains the most complete list of Jarry's works as well as many interesting documents on Jarry.

Sutton, Lewis Franklin. "An Evaluation of Studies on Alfred Jarry from 1894-1963." Unpublished Diss., University of North Carolina, 1966.

B. BOOKS

Chassé, Charles. *Dans les coulisses de la gloire: d'Ubu-Roi au Douanier Rousseau.* Paris: Editions de la Nouvelle Revue Critique, 1947.

Chauveau, Paul. *Alfred Jarry ou la naissance, la vie et la mort du Père Ubu.* 5th ed. Paris: Mercure de France, 1932.

Connolly, Cyril. *Ideas and Places.* New York: Harper and Bros., 1953.

LeBois, André. *Alfred Jarry l'irremplaçable.* Paris: Le Cercle du Livre, 1950.

Levesque, Jacques-Henry. *Alfred Jarry.* Poètes d'aujourd'hui. Paris: Editions Pierre Seghers, 1951.

Lot, Fernand. *Alfred Jarry, son œuvre. Portrait et autographe.* Paris: Editions de la Nouvelle Revue Critique, 1934.

Morienval, Jean. *De Pathelin à Ubu, le Bilan des types littéraires*. Paris: Librairie Bloud et Gay, n. d.

Perche, Louis. *Alfred Jarry*. Classiques du XXᵉ siècle. Paris: Editions Universitaires, 1965.

Rachilde, [Marguerite Eymery Vallette]. *Alfred Jarry ou le Surmâle de lettres*. La Vie de Bohème. Paris: Bernard Grasset, 1928.

Shattuck, Roger. *The Banquet Years. The Arts in France, 1885-1918*. New York: Harcourt, Brace & Co., 1955.

C. ARTICLES

Les Cahiers du Collège de 'Pataphysique and the later series *Les Dossiers du Collège* contain numerous articles on Jarry and *Ubu Roi*. See especially 1-2, 3-4, 5-6, 10, and 20.

Les Marges, 23 (January 15, 1922). The issue was dedicated to Jarry and contained articles by Apollinaire, Fagus, C. Gandilhon Gens-d'Armes, Eugène Montfort, and Dr. Jean Saltas.

Arrivé, Michel. "Structuration et destructuration du signe dans quelques textes de Jarry." In *Essais de sémiotique poétique*. Paris: Larousse, 1972.

Bauer, Gérard. "Les Théâtres: *Ubu Roi* au Vieux Colombier." *Revue de Paris*, 4 (January, 1947), 163.

Beaubourg, Maurice. "*Ubu Roi* aux Quat-Z-Arts." *La Plume*, 13 (July-December, 1901), 1029-1030.

Bedner, Jules. "Eléments guignolesques dans le théâtre d'Alfred Jarry." *Revue d'Histoire Littéraire de la France*, 73 (1973), 69-84.

Béhar, Henri. "De l'inversion des signes dans *Ubu enchaîné*," *Etudes Françaises*, 7 (1971), 3-21.

Boissard, Maurice [Paul Léautaud]. "Chronique Dramatique: *Ubu-Roi* par Alfred Jarry." *Nouvelle Revue Française*, 17 (December, 1921), 730-732.

———. "Chronique Dramatique: Théâtre de l'Œuvre: *Ubu-Roi* d'Alfred Jarry." *Nouvelle Revue Française*, 18 (Jan.-June, 1922), 593-595.

Breton, André. "Alfred Jarry." *Les Ecrits Nouveaux*, 3 (January, 1919), 17-27.

Brisson, Adolphe. "Alfred Jarry: Théâtre Gémier: *Ubu Roi* (reprise)." *Le Théâtre*. 3ᵉ série. Paris: Librairie des Annales, n. d.

Case, Jules. "*Ubu Roi*." *La Nouvelle Revue*, (September 15, 1896), 428.

———. "*Ubu Roi*." *La Nouvelle Revue*, (January 1, 1897), 198.

Chassé, Charles. "*L'Affaire Ubu*." *La Grande Revue*, 109 (August, 1922), 241-263.

———. "Le Vocabulaire de Jarry dans *Ubu Roi*." *C.A.I.E.F.*, 11 (May, 1959), 363-367.

Chauveau, Paul. "Alfred Jarry." *Revue de Paris*, 5 (October 1, 1938), 612-624.

———. "Notes sur Alfred Jarry." *Mercure de France*, 191 (November 1, 1926), 581-599.

Dumur, Louis. "*Ubu Roi*." *Mercure de France*, 19 (September, 1896), 544-546.

Eekhoud, Georges. "Chronique de Bruxelles." *Mercure de France*, 42 (June, 1902), 836-837.

———. "Chronique de Bruxelles: Souvenirs sur Alfred Jarry en Belgique." *Mercure de France*, 70 (Dec., 1906), 556.

Fontainas, André. "Les Poèmes." *Mercure de France*, 155 (April-May, 1922), 752-754.

Gassler, Eve. "Legend of Ubu." *Bard Review,* 2 (1948), 149-155.

Gide, André. "Le Groupement littéraire qu'abritait le *Mercure de France.*" *Mercure de France,* 298 (Dec., 1946), 168-170.

Gourmont, Jean de. "Littérature: (Alfred Jarry — *Ubu Roi.* Fasquelle — *Sous le Masque d'Alfred Jarry. Les Sources d'Ubu Roi* par Charles Chassé, Floury)." *Mercure de France,* 155 (April 1, 1922), 151-154.

————. "Littérature (Laurent Tailhade: *Quelques fantômes de jadis.*)" *Mercure de France,* 141 (August 1, 1920), 789-790.

Gourmont, Remy de. "Les Livres: *Les Minutes de Sable Mémorial,* par Alfred Jarry." *Mercure de France,* 12 (October, 1894), 177-178.

G. S. "Les Théâtres." *L'Illustration,* No. 4122 (March 4, 1922), 211.

Grossman, Manuel L. "Alfred Jarry and the Theater of the Absurd." *Educational Theater Journal,* 109, No. 4 (December, 1967), 473-477.

Hérold, A. Ferdinand. "Théâtre: *Ubu Roi.*" *Mercure de France,* 21 (January, 1897), 217-219.

Hirsch, Charles Henri. "Les Revues: (*Les Marges*: M. Fagus et G. Apollinaire, à propos d'Alfred Jarry. Alfred Jarry avant le succès d'Ubu)." *Mercure de France,* 154 (March 1, 1922), 479-481.

Interim. "Théâtre. *Ubu Roi* (reprise)." *Mercure de France,* 155 (April-May, 1922), 163.

Königsberg, I. "New Light on Alfred Jarry's Juvenilia." *Modern Language Quarterly,* 27 (September, 1966), 299-305.

Lemarchand, Jacques. "Ubu au Soleil." *La Nouvelle Nouvelle Revue Française,* 6ᵉ année (April-June, 1958), 891-894.

Lugné-Poe, A. F. "A propos de 'l'Inutilité du théâtre au théâtre.' " *Mercure de France,* 20 (October, 1896), 90-98.

————. "La Semaine Théâtrale — A propos d'*Ubu Roi.*" *L'Eclair* (January 10, 1922), 3.

Pierrefeu, Jean de. "Le Cas d'*Ubu Roi.*" *Journal des Débats,* 28 (Dec. 30, 1921), 1144-1146.

Quillard, Pierre. "L'Infaillibilité du sabre." *Mercure de France,* 25 (February, 1898), 353-365.

Rachilde [Marguerite Eymery Vallette]. "Roman: *L'Amour en visites.*" *Mercure de France,* 26 (June, 1898), 834-835.

————. "Roman: *Les Jours et les nuits.*" *Mercure de France,* 23 (July, 1897), 143-145.

————. "Roman: *Le Surmâle.*" *Mercure de France,* 42 (June, 1902), 753-755.

Rainey, Brian E. "Alfred Jarry and Ubu: The 'Fin de Siècle' en France." *Wascana Review,* 4 (1969), 28-36.

Rémond, Georges. "Souvenirs sur Jarry et autres." *Mercure de France,* 323 (1955), 427-446, 656-677.

Salmon, André. "Alfred Jarry ou le Père Ubu en liberté." *L'Ami du Lettré* (1924), 239-264.

St. Prix, Pierre de. "A la recherche de la paternité d'Ubu. L'Opinion du docteur Jean Saltas." *Ere Nouvelle,* 42ᵉ année (January 17, 1922), 3.

Shattuck, Roger. "Le Type et le tic." Introduction to Alfred Jarry, *L'Objet aimé.* Paris: Arcanes, 1953. Pp. 9-26.

Sinclair, Andrew. "So Ubu to You." *Time and Tide,* 42 (November, 1961), 2018.

Taylor, A. Carey. "Le Vocabulaire d'Alfred Jarry." *C.A.I.E.F.*, 11 (May, 1959), 307-322.

Thérive, André. "Le Mystère d'*Ubu Roi*." *L'Opinion*, 14ᵉ année, No. 50 (December 10, 1921), 651-652.

Vallette, Alfred. "Echos: Sépulture d'Alfred Jarry." *Mercure de France*, 70 (December 1, 1906), 574.

Vandérem, Fernand. "Les Lettres et la vie." *Revue de France* (March 15, 1922), 387-405.

van Roosbroeck, G. L. "Alfred Jarry: The Genesis of *Ubu Roi*." *Romanic Review*, 25 (1934), 415-417.

Verhaeren, Emile. "Les Marionnettes." *L'Art Moderne*, 16, No. 29 (July 19, 1896), 228-229.

Wellwarth, George. "Seed of the Avant-Garde." *Criticism*, 4 (Spring, 1962), 108-119.

Weightman, John. "Beyond the Fringe." *New York Review of Books*, 5, No. 6 (October 28, 1965), 8-12.

York, Ruth B. "Ubu Revisited. The Reprise of 1922." *French Review*, 25 (February, 1962), 408-411.

Z. "Les Sources d'*Ubu Roi*." *Journal des Débats*, 28 (December 9, 1921), 1011-1012.

INDEX

"Affaire Ubu," 9, 32ff.
Alazon, 60.
Antoine and Le Théâtre Libre, 17.
Apollinaire, Guillaume, 21.
Apparition scene, the, 54-56, 64, 66, 100-103.
Artaud, Antonin, 10, 21.
"Autre présentation *d'Ubu Roi* par l'auteur," 70, 78, 107.

"Bataille d'Hernani, le," 15.
Battles and combats, 53-54, 56, 97-98.
Bauer, Henry, 8, 19-20.
Bear scene, the, 52, 54-55, 60, 64, 73, 98-100.
Bergson, Henri, 110.
Bonnard, Pierre, 16, 31.
Bordure, 48ff., 62-63, 66, 77-78.
Bougrelas, 48ff., 66, 78, 94, 96, 106.
Burlesque, 18, 75, 85ff.

César-Antéchrist, 30, 77, 105.
"Chanson du décervelage, la," 63, 76-77.
Chassé, Charles, 9, 30ff.
Cocteau, Jean, 21.
Collège de 'Pataphysique, le, 10, 44, 45.
Colloquialisms, 84-87.
Conspirator's dinner, the, 51-52.
Copeau, Jacques, 20.
Cycles ubiques, les, 24, 26, 60, 63, 105, 107.
Czar of Russia, 49, 54, 61, 74, 98.

Dernier supplice, le, 63, 89, 90, 94-95.

"Douze arguments sur le théâtre," 109.
"Du mimétisme inverse chez les personnages de Henri de Régnier," 69-70.

En attendant Godot, 110.

Falstaff, 60, 64, 66-67.
"Fantaisie verbale, la," 75-76, 92ff.
Fort, Paul, 38, 39.
Fouquier, Henry, 19-20.

Gargantua, 19, 60, 64.
Gemier, Firmin, 16.
Gidouille, 17-18, 60, 81, 83.
"Guignol," 29, 44.
Guignolesque elements, 15-in quote, 17, 18-19, 40, 47, 56, 60, 69, 71, 94, 106, 107, 110.

Hamlet, 38, 51, 97.
Harpagon, 62.

"De l'inutilité du théâtre au théâtre," 107.
Ionesco, Eugène, 11, 112.

"Jarry sur la Butte," 45-46.
Julius Caesar, 51.

Letter of Alfred Jarry to Lugné-Poe, 18, 30, 52, 69, 106.
Letter of Charles Morin to Henry Bauer, 34.
Letter of Stéphane Mallarmé to Alfred Jarry, 20.
Lugné-Poe, 18, 30, 39-41.

Macbeth, 51, 57.
Maître des Finances, 48, 68, 82, 91.
Mallarmé, Stéphane, 20, 105.
Mask, 15, 69-70, 106, 108, 111.
Mercure de France, Le, 29, 33, 38.
"Merdre," 16, 36, 79-80, 82-83.
Mère Ubu, 18, 46, 72-73.
Miles gloriosus, 60.
Minutes de Sables Mémorial, Les, 30, 105.
Mock-heroic, 51, 53, 96-97.
Morin, Charles and Henri, 24, 25, 33ff., 76.

Nègres, Les, 111.
Neologisms, 36-37, 79-81.

Obscenity, 18, 27, 64, 82-84, 105, 111.
"Onésime ou les Tribulations de Priou," 26, 44.

Palotins, 27, 55, 64, 73-74, 78.
Pantomime, 51ff.
Panurge, 38, 60.
"Paralipomènes d'Ubu, Les," 17-18, 31, 59, 70, 77, 107.
"Parler Ubu, le," 18, 75ff.
Parody, 17, 47ff., 75, 105.
'Pataphysique, La, 26 note.
Perhinderion, 29 note, 35 note.
Pirandello, Luigi, *Maschere nude,* 111.
Polichinelle, 60, 64.
"Polonais, Les," 25, 33ff., 76, 78, 95-96.
"Polyèdes, Les," 30, 31.
"Preliminary Address," 15-16, 18, 23, 59, 69, 107.
Professeur Hébert, le, 23, 59, 76, 105.

Queen Rosemonde, 74, 94.
"Questions de théâtre," 59, 65, 71, 89, 108-109.

Rabelais, 19, 24, 60, 72, 81, 92 note.
Rachilde (Marguerite Eymery Vallette), 9, 20, 29, 71-72.

Sarcey, Francisque, 19.
Satire, 47, 56-57, 67-68, 70ff., 104.
Savage God, the, 17, 112.
Schwob, Marcel, 20, 29, 38.
Shakespeare, 24, 50-51, 57, 72, 74.
Symbolist Movement, the, 29, 35-43, 105, 109-110.

Tartuffe, 38, 66.
Terrasse, Claude, 31, 41.
Théâtre Alfred Jarry, Le, 21.
Théâtre de l'Œuvre, Le, 15, 30, 40, 78, 106.
Théâtre des Phynances, Le, 31, 81.
Theater of the Absurd, The, 10-11, 12, 111-112.

Ubu Cocu, 29-30, 31, 32, 43, 44, 57, 63 note, 65, 67-68, 107.
"Ubu Cocu ou l'Archéoptéryx," 44, 63.
Ubu enchaîné, 32, 43, 44, 57.
Ubu Roi
    Editions, 30, 31, 37, 44, 46.
    Performances, 15-19, 31, 32, 40-43, 44, 45, 46.
    Translations, 44, 45.
Ubu sur la Butte, 32.

Vallette, Alfred, 9, 29.
Venceslas, 47-50, 65, 74, 78, 96.
Violence, 18, 27, 63-64, 89-90, 105, 111.

Yeats, William Butler, 16, 112.
Ymagier, L', 29, 77.